EDIBLES
FOR BEGINNERS

EDIBLES
FOR BEGINNERS
A CANNABIS COOKBOOK

LAURIE WOLF AND MARY WOLF

callisto
publishing
an imprint of Sourcebooks

Copyright © 2019 by Callisto Publishing LLC
Cover and internal design © 2019 by Callisto Publishing LLC
Photography: Cover and all interior photography except for page xiv © 2019 Marija Vidal, with food styling by Elisabet der Nederlanden; © Lew Robertson/Stock Pot Images, p. xiv.
Cover Designer: Diana Haas
Interior Designer: John Clifford
Art Producer: Sue Bischofberger
Editor: Pam Kingsley
Production Editor: Ashley Polikoff

Published by Callisto Publishing LLC C/O Sourcebooks LLC
P.O. Box 4410, Naperville, Illinois 60567-4410
(630) 961-3900
callistopublishing.com

Printed and bound in China
OGP 3

This book is dedicated to all the patients,
doctors, and advocates who devote their time and energy
to the decriminalization, legalization,
and destigmatization of cannabis.

CONTENTS

INTRODUCTION

The concept of a cannabis edible can seem magical and mystifying to a beginner. How do you get it in the food? How do you know how potent it will be? How will it affect you or others? How do you make it taste good? Once we walk you through the basics in this book, I promise you will be equipped with enough knowledge to confidently make your own cannabis edibles.

Edibles have come a long way from the basic pot brownie—although, if I'm being honest, a cannabis-infused brownie is still pretty incredible.

Chocolate and cannabis work so well together. As you start on your journey of infusing foods with cannabis, you'll start to notice some of those winning combinations. But these days we infuse everything from Brussels sprouts and sliders to ice pops and pavlova.

The beauty of homemade edibles lies in the ability to control and personalize your creations—whether you are nut-free, gluten-free, vegan, or Paleo. And making your own infusions allows you to control your potency and build confidence in knowing what the effects will be.

I began making edibles years ago, while I was in college. They were the standard brownies and crisped rice treats, and it was always a crapshoot as to their potency and taste. There were two strain choices, Acapulco Gold and Panama Red, and the quality of the cannabis varied widely. Most of the time the edibles did their job, but there was no consistency and overdoing it was common. If you have ever overindulged in a cannabis edible, you know that the experience is quite unpleasant, and if it's your first time, it might put you off the plant indefinitely. I don't want that to happen to you, so all the recipes in this book are developed to be low dose, no more than 5mg per serving.

Once you learn the steps of infusing oil and butter with cannabis, you can pretty much make anything your hungry heart desires. As long as the recipe has a fat, you can add THC or CBD to it and impress yourself and your friends with an edible you can trust. No guessing, no overdoing it. I mean, you will have to exercise self-control, but if you know the potency and the size of a dose, you have no one but yourself to blame for that miserable few hours if you do overindulge (see page 42 for what you can do if you find yourself in that situation).

When it comes to edibles, and cannabis in general, less is more, and when you reach your sweet spot, stay there. And stay home. Never drive while under the influence, do not offer edibles to people under age, and never give edibles to people without their knowledge. And label, label, label your infusions. I can't stress that enough.

When I started my edible company in 2012, I was determined to make cannabis-infused treats that were consistent, made from top-quality ingredients, and delicious. Back then that was quite a challenge. My goal was to make a product that was more than a vehicle for getting high. I wanted people to say that they would be happy to eat my edibles just for their taste.

Today, with Mary, our company, Laurie + MaryJane, has 10 employees, we are in over 300 dispensaries, and have won multiple awards for our edibles. We source our cannabis from organic farms with stellar reputations. The lab we use, Green Leaf, has allowed us to perfect our potency dosing, and we offer consistently tasty treats that people adore. Making edibles is fun—eating edibles is better. I am a cannabis lover and enjoy partaking in almost every method.

That said, I love eating an edible and feeling the subtle indications that it is starting to take effect. The experience is a more all-over head and body feel, and it doesn't get old. I do, but it doesn't.

Whether you are interested in cannabis-infused edibles for medical reasons, recreational ones, or just for the novelty, it is a pretty fun activity that brings together art and science. A love of baking and cooking is all you really need to get started. We've compiled and distilled our expertise in all things edibles into this guide to get you started with creating your own homemade edibles safely and effectively.

I hope you enjoy this guide and find it helpful in beginning your edible adventures!

—Laurie Wolf

PART

GETTING STARTED

CHAPTER 1

Cannabis 101

Chances are if you are picking up a book on how to make edibles, you already have some knowledge of the cannabis plant. Whether you experimented in college or have more recently enjoyed the effects of cannabis in your life, it is always important to start with the basics. Knowing the parts of the plant, how and why it affects us, and how and why inhaling it varies from ingesting it is vital when getting started with making your own cannabis infusions safely and effectively. And believe us, this part is pretty fascinating. You won't want to skip it.

THE PLANT

Let's start with a primer on cannabis terminology and anatomy. Working your way up from the soil, starting with the stem of the plant, you'll begin to see fan leaves (the iconic marijuana leaf) up until the main bud, or cola. This is the flower. Smaller buds grow from the nodes between fan leaves. The buds are made up of calyxes, which contain the highest concentration of trichomes, or plant resin. Extending past the calyxes are tiny orange hairs—the pistils. All you really need to know about pistils is that they play an important role in the plant's reproduction.

The flower/bud is what people smoke. Though iconic, the fan leaves of the plant are the least potent and usually just tossed out at harvest. Smaller leaves that are close to the buds are sugar leaves, or trim leaves. These are great to use in infusions/extracts. Just like the flowers, they are coated in trichomes. The stem is very low in potency but is thought to have a decent concentration of CBD.

If you walked into a cannabis dispensary today, chances are you'd be presented with three or more categories of cannabis flower: sativa, indica, and hybrids, which may be further categorized into sativa-dominant hybrid, indica-dominant hybrid, or split hybrids. However, the distinction of sativa versus indica is quickly losing its importance. When researchers analyzed nearly 500 strains, they found no evidence that the "indicas" were chemically distinct from the "sativas." The emerging opinion today is that the range of effects produced from different cannabis strains comes down to the ratio of cannabinoids and terpenes, the chemical compounds found in the plant's resin. It will be interesting to see how the categorization of the strains develops.

SATIVA

Sativa strains tend to yield tall plants that are high in THC and have long, finger-like leaves. They are known for giving stimulating, creative "head" highs filled with laughter and in-depth conversations. On the flip side, they have also been known to increase feelings of anxiety and paranoia. Some sativa strains are thought to enhance lights and sounds, making them great for enjoying music, movies, or the outdoors. Popular sativas include Sour Diesel, Green Crack, Jack Herer, Durban Poison, and Lemon Haze.

INDICA

Indica strains are shorter, stockier, and have wide leaves. They tend to flower faster than sativas and produce a higher yield. Indicas are known for producing a more relaxing, full-body experience that's ideal for the treatment of pain, muscle spasms, anxiety, nausea, loss of appetite, and sleep. Some effects have been described as "couch lock," which can be good or bad depending on how you see it. Popular indicas include Bubba Kush, Northern Lights, Purple Kush, Blueberry, and G13.

HYBRIDS

Each season, growers develop new hybrids by crossbreeding select strains to produce a whole new variety tailored to meet desired effects. Hybrids cover a vast area in the crossbreeding of sativas and indicas, creating specialty strains that are bred for specific traits from each species. Many of the most-loved strains are hybrids, like Blue Dream, Girl Scout Cookies (GSC), OG Kush, Pineapple Express, and Trainwreck.

CANNABINOIDS

The plant's resin contains hundreds of chemical compounds in the form of cannabinoids and terpenes. When the cannabinoids enter the bloodstream, they activate cannabinoid receptors throughout the endocannabinoid system in our bodies, producing a range of effects. Cannabinoid receptors are found throughout the human body: They are in the brain, organs, central and peripheral nervous system, cardiovascular system, reproductive system, gastrointestinal system, urinary system, immune system, and even cartilage. The endocannabinoid system regulates the homeostasis of our biological functions—appetite, memory, metabolism, female reproduction, sleep, immune response, thermoregulation, pain, autonomic nervous system, and stress response—and is considered the most important system in the human body.

Let's say that one more time—it is considered the most important system in the human body. Our bodies naturally make endocannabinoids to stimulate the cannabinoid receptors and regulate the system. Cannabinoids such as THC and

CBD are external substances that stimulate these same receptors. This certainly explains how cannabis can provide such a range of benefits across a vast array of conditions and illnesses. Research indicates that the introduction of external cannabinoids like THC can cause the endocannabinoid system to create more receptors and increase an individual's future sensitivity to the cannabinoids. Conversely, the endocannabinoid system has also been shown to restrict the number of receptors when it experiences an overabundance of cannabinoids.

An interesting side note here: Research shows that taking a break from cannabis for 28 days (also known as a tolerance break), can reset the body's endocannabinoid system to its pre-cannabis state. This self-regulation makes sense for a system known to control the body's homeostasis.

THC/THCA

THC, tetrahydrocannabinol, is the most well-known cannabinoid, and appropriately so, in our opinion. It is not only responsible for the beloved psychoactive effects but also for relieving pain, nausea, lack of appetite, and inflammation. THC mimics the cannabinoids naturally produced in the body and activates receptors in the brain associated with thinking, pain, pleasure, time perception, coordination, and concentration. It binds to cannabinoid receptors in the central nervous system and the immune system, resulting in relaxation, reduced pain, and increased appetite, which is responsible for giving us a case of the "munchies." THC also appears to protect the brain by reducing inflammation and stimulating neurogenesis.

In raw cannabis, you will find THCA instead of THC. Once heated (decarboxylated), THCA becomes THC. THCA is non-psychoactive and brings its own set of medicinal benefits. It has anti-proliferative and anti-inflammatory abilities and appears to help chronic immune system disorders. THCA has been used to treat cancer, muscle spasms, seizures, lupus, arthritis, endometriosis, and menstrual cramps. Raw plants can be juiced for THCA. Non-heated tinctures can also be made with high levels of THCA.

CBD/CBDA

Quickly gaining popularity is the now federally legal cannabidiol, CBD. It seems like you can't walk two blocks without seeing a sign for it these days. CBD is the second most common cannabinoid and acts on different receptors throughout the body than THC, so there are little, if any, psychotropic results. Studies have shown that CBD offers pain relief and has anti-inflammatory and anti-anxiety properties. Research is now focusing on CBD in its treatment of epilepsy, Crohn's disease, PTSD, and multiple sclerosis, just to name a few. CBD has also been shown to reduce the effects of THC, which in large quantities can be very unpleasant. Like THC, CBD starts as a different cannabinoid, CBDA, and must be heated (decarboxylated) to convert it into CBD. CBDA may be helpful as an anti-convulsant and to relieve nausea, pain, and inflammation. It may even have cancer-preventing properties. CBDA can be obtained through raw CBD-dominant strains.

CBG

Cannabigerol (CBG) is also growing in importance. CBG is non-psychoactive and responsible for the production of both THC and CBD. Plants that are harvested three-quarters of the way through the flowering cycle may preserve some CBG. A strain that is high in CBG (around 1 percent) is Harlequin. CBG has sedating, antimicrobial, antioxidant, and anti-inflammatory properties and can treat IBS, glaucoma (by lowering intraocular pressure), and insomnia. It has also been shown to kill cancer cells and inhibit tumor growth.

CBN

CBN is created when THC is exposed to light and oxygen. It can cause an intense body high and make consumers dizzy or groggy. It has mild psychoactive effects and appears to increase the effects of THC. Its medicinal effects include reducing epilepsy and muscle spasms, relieving intraocular pressure, and reducing depression. All strains can produce CBN when exposed to light and oxygen. It may also be possible to find CBN-rich products at your local dispensary.

Medical Cannabis

Cannabis has a wide range of powerful health benefits. People have been growing and using cannabis medicinally for thousands of years. Records as far back as 2700 BCE show over 100 uses for cannabis, including the treatment of gout, rheumatism, malaria, and absentmindedness. New research continues to emerge and confirm the efficacy of modern and centuries-old therapies. Although scientists are optimistic that marijuana will prove to be helpful in treating many serious illnesses, and perhaps even a cure, there is a need for more clinical study.

For THC to work best, medical experts suggest taking it with a little CBD. Similarly, for CBD to be most effective, a little THC is suggested as well.

Conditions THC has been shown to provide relief for:

Pain

HIV/AIDS

Muscle spasticity

Fibromyalgia

Glaucoma

Insomnia and sleep disorders

Loss of appetite and nausea

Anxiety, stress, PTSD

Epilepsy

Asthma

Dependency on and withdrawal from opiates and alcohol

Neurodegeneration, including Alzheimer's and Parkinson's diseases and stroke

Acute head trauma

Amyotrophic lateral sclerosis (ALS)

Inflammatory bowel disease (IBS) and Crohn's disease

Migraines and headaches

Conditions CBD has been shown to provide relief from:

Seizures and epileptic disorders

Inflammation and pain

IBS and Crohn's disease

Nausea

Migraines and headaches

Depression, psychosis, and mood disorders

Anxiety, stress, PTSD

Multiple sclerosis (MS)

Opioid withdrawal

Attention deficit hyperactivity disorder (ADHD)

ALS

Asthma

Autism

Cancer

Neurodegeneration, including Alzheimer's and Parkinson's diseases and stroke

Alcohol-induced brain damage

TERPENES

You may notice distinct aromas across various strains of cannabis. The complex flavor profiles and signature smells of different cannabis strains come from their terpenes. Like cannabinoids, terpenes are excreted in the trichome resin and contribute to the overall effects of the plant. But unlike cannabinoids, terpenes are not only in cannabis—they are present in many of our everyday foods, flowers, and herbs, like lemon, mint, lavender, and berries. They are what give cannabis strains their unique aromas and flavors, and may tell you more about a particular strain's effects than the name or categorization. Pinene smells of, well, pine, and promotes alertness. Myrcene, found in mango and thyme, smells earthy and tropical and is very sedating. Limonene is citrusy and a mood elevator.

Although recent research has focused on the cannabinoids of marijuana, terpenes are the next frontier. There are over 200 different terpenes found in cannabis, and the terpenes profile of a particular strain is believed to play a very significant role in that strain's effects. Gone are the days of judging a strain by its THC percentage and indica versus sativa. Now you must use your nose.

Terpenes have a wide range of effects, parallel to the prized medicinal uses of cannabis: anti-inflammatory, pain relief, anti-anxiety, anti-epileptic, etc. Emerging research has discovered that terpenes work with cannabinoids synergistically (I hate this word, but nowhere is it more appropriate) to contribute to the overall medicinal effect of a strain. Researchers have termed this "the entourage effect." In trying to develop drugs based off cannabinoids, pharmaceutical companies found that whole plant extracts worked better than isolated compounds, or that the whole is greater than the sum of its parts.

During the decarboxylation, infusion, and cooking process, many terpenes are lost, but if you infuse low and slow, you can retain a decent amount of the plant's terpene profile. If you understand the flavor of your cannabis, you can know how to best pair it with your food. Really smell your cannabis and let the taste linger. Understanding the aroma and taste of terpenes can make you a true "cannasseur."

CARYOPHYLLENE

Caryophyllene has been described as a terpene that acts like a cannabinoid. It turns out caryophyllene interacts with the endocannabinoid system on the same receptor as CBD.

Flavors/Aromas: Rich, peppery, spicy, woody

Found in/Pairs well with: Thai basil, cloves, black pepper, caraway, oregano, lavender, rosemary, cinnamon, hops

Strains: Hash Plant, Super Silver Haze, Candyland, Death Star, Girl Scout Cookies (GSC)

Effects/Uses: Antiseptic, antibacterial, antifungal, anti-inflammatory; good for arthritis, ulcers, autoimmune disorders, and other gastrointestinal complications

HUMULENE

Did you know that cannabis and hops are closely related? Humulene is the terpene responsible for giving both a similar aromatic, hoppy profile.

Flavors/Aromas: Hops, earthy, musky, spicy

Found in/Pairs well with: Basil, sage, clove, ginger, ginseng

Strains: ACDC, Banana Kush, Durban Poison, OG Kush, Trainwreck

Effects/Uses: Antibacterial, anti-inflammatory, antifungal, analgesic

LIMONENE

Next to myrcene, limonene is the most abundant terpene in cannabis and leads the "entourage" by increasing the absorption of other terpenes.

Flavors/Aromas: Bright, citrusy

Found in/Pairs well with: Citrus rind, rosemary, juniper, peppermint

Strains: OG Kush, Super Lemon Haze, Lemon Skunk

Effects/Uses: Elevated mood, stress relief, antifungal, antibacterial, anticarcinogenic; fights gastric reflux, gastrointestinal issues, gallstones, depression, and anxiety

LINALOOL

Once you start looking, you'll notice that linalool is frequently used for its scent in many skincare products. Linalool is naturally occurring in flowers and spices like basil and lavender.

Flavor/Aroma: Floral, citrus notes, sweet, candy-like

Found in/Pairs well with: Lavender, citrus, rosewood, coriander, mint, cinnamon, coriander, basil

Strains: G13, LA Confidential, Lavender

Effects/Uses: Antipsychotic, anti-epileptic, anti-anxiety, anti-acne, sedative, pain relief, antidepressant

MYRCENE

Myrcene, the most profuse terpene in cannabis, is perhaps also the most important terpene—its presence is said to determine if a strain is indica or sativa. Plants with 0.5 percent or more myrcene are said to be indica and less than 0.5 percent are said to be sativa. The sedating, relaxing effects of myrcene clearly play a big role in the experience of a strain. An enduring anecdote with cannabis-food pairing is to eat a mango before or while smoking to increase its effects. The reasoning here is that the myrcene in mangos helps the passage of THC through the blood-brain barrier.

Flavor/Aroma: Musky, earthy, herbal with notes of citrus and tropical fruit

Found in/Pairs well with: Mango, hops, bay leaves, lemongrass, eucalyptus, thyme, basil

Strains: White Widow, Harlequin, Pure Kush, Skunk #1

Effects/Uses: Sedating, relaxing, pain relief, anti-spasm, anti-inflammatory, anti-insomnia, antibiotic

NEROLIDOL

This terpene improves transdermal absorption, making it a great additive to topicals.

Flavors/Aromas: Woody, fresh bark, floral

Found in/Pairs well with: Ginger, lavender, lemongrass, jasmine, orange, tea tree

Strains: Jack Herer, Skywalker OG, Sour Diesel, Island Sweet Skunk, Girl Scout Cookies (GSC), Blue Dream

Effects/Uses: Antioxidant, antifungal, anticancer, antimicrobial, sedative

PINENE

This piney terpene is pretty easy to identify. And with its ability to improve short-term memory, you'll be able to remember you identified it!

Flavors/Aromas: Sweet, pine

Found in/Pairs well with: Pine, rosemary, basil, parsley, dill, orange

Strains: Jack Herer, Chemdawg, Bubba Kush, Trainwreck, Super Silver Haze

Effects/Uses: Asthma relief, anti-inflammatory, alertness, memory retention, may counteract THC effects

TERPINOLENE

Like linalool, terpinolene is frequently used in fragranced items due to its pleasing smell.

Flavors/Aromas: Woody, smoky, fresh, piney, herbal, floral

Found in/Pairs well with: Apples, cumin, tea tree, nutmeg

Strains: Mostly exclusive to sativas like Super Lemon Haze, Jack Herer

Effects/Uses: Antifungal, antibacterial, anti-insomnia, antioxidant, anticarcinogenic, sedative

CHAPTER 2

A Flavor Guide to Selected Strains

This chapter lists the most popular (and our favorite) strains to use when making an infusion. We tend to cook with what we like to smoke because we know the flavor as well as the effects. We'll explore strains and what makes them tick. Although the labels "hybrid," "sativa," and "indica" are listed according to these traditional categorizations, we find that the terpene and cannabinoid profiles in each strain are more influential to the strain's effect.

The average proportion of THC and CBD content is listed for each strain, but this can vary with the strains you find. Be aware that environmental factors such as temperature, sunlight, soil type, and food/nutrients can affect the final output and effects of a plant— sometimes wildly. So, although each strain has pretty set genetics, don't be surprised if Bubba Kush from one grower is not quite same as Bubba Kush from another.

BLUEBERRY DIESEL (AKA BLUE DIESEL)

60% INDICA / 40% SATIVA

A descendant of the famous strains Blueberry and Sour Diesel, this popular hybrid is best known for its aroma of (surprise!) blueberry and diesel fuel. It can provide a mellow mixture of mental and physical relaxation thanks to its indica lineage, and users have noted substantial mental stimulation coming from its sativa side. This is a great everyday strain that infuses well and is very versatile.

THC: 20.5%

CBD: 0%

Flavor Profile: You'll notice a strong scent of blueberry, giving off a fruity and tangy aroma with a hint of astringent fuel. In an infusion, it gives a slightly fruity, herbal, and bitter taste. The mix of caryophyllene, myrcene, humulene, and limonene makes this terpene profile work for foods that are sweet with spicy notes.

Health Benefits: This versatile strain can help treat insomnia, anxiety disorder, loss of appetite, depression, pain, and migraines. It's soothing, uplifting, and clarifying. While some people like it in the daytime to manage pain with an uplifting experience, others like to enjoy the strain at night to provide stress relief and sedation for a good night's sleep.

BLUE DREAM

60% SATIVA / 40% INDICA

A great-tasting hybrid, Blue Dream produces full-body relaxation with a calm euphoria. Originating in California, it is increasingly popular nationwide. Those new and returning to Blue Dream have noted the enjoyable level of effects, including a relaxed but swift relief to symptoms such as pain or depression without heavy sedative effects. Blue Dream is a solid choice for those seeking a daytime medicine.

THC: 17%–24%

CBD: 0.1%–0.2%

Flavor Profile: A sweet, herbal, floral, and fruity strain with tangs of blueberry, mango, and vanilla. Dominant terpenes in this strain are myrcene, pinene, caryophyllene, and terpinolene. We love to infuse tropical desserts, especially mangos, with Blue Dream.

Health Benefits: This classic hybrid is loved for creating relaxation and euphoria while acting as an appetite stimulant and treating depression, migraines, nausea, pain, sleep disorders, and stress.

BRUCE BANNER #3

60% SATIVA / 40% INDICA

This appropriately named strain packs a punch with a concentration of THC reaching nearly 30 percent. As a sativa-dominant hybrid, Bruce Banner #3 is the most coveted of five Banner buds developed by Dark Horse Genetics. The effects come on strong before mellowing into a creative euphoria, relaxing the body and leaving a big smile on your face. If you are looking to optimize the potency of your infusion, Bruce Banner #3 reliably yields *high* results.

THC: 24%–30%

CBD: 0.5%–1.0%

Flavor Profile: Earthy, citrusy, piney, and sour aromas interwoven with musk and diesel. We like to use Bruce Banner #3 on savory dishes filled with fresh herbs (particularly lemon thyme and sage), like stuffed mushroom caps.

Health Benefits: Used to manage anxiety and stress while treating everyday aches and pains. Bruce Banner #3 can also help treat ADHD, arthritis, bipolar disorder, pain, cramps, and migraines.

BUBBA KUSH

80% INDICA / 20% SATIVA

Choose Bubba Kush and you will be delivered with head-to-toe relaxation. With reviewers remarking on its tranquilizing effects, users are met with waves of euphoria, leaving stress and anxiety at the shore, delivering a welcomed sleepiness. Look for a dense bud structure, featuring hues of forest green to pale purple.

THC: 14%–22%

CBD: 0.0%–0.01%

Flavor Profile: Bubba Kush delivers sweet, slightly spicy, herbal, and floral tones interwoven with chocolate, coffee, and nutty favors. It's got a bit of just about everything, making for an excellent, versatile infusion.

Health Benefits: Find relief from depression, insomnia, pain, stress, and lack of appetite with this sedating and relaxing strain. It's a favorite of a bunch of my friends when looking for a true relaxation from daily woes.

CHEMDAWG

HYBRID

Winner of four awards, Chemdawg has a mysterious origin and unclear genetics. It is a potent strain, linked to strong cerebral experiences, coupled with a powerful heavy-bodied feeling. There is a mental rush at the onset, which morphs into an impressive body high with an overall uplifting experience.

THC: 15%–26%

CBD: 0.0%–1.5%

Flavor Profile: Chemdawg is known for being super pungent with earthy, diesel aromas. I'll be honest—the smell can sometimes be a bit overwhelming, but it has an interesting complexity. We like to use this strain in savory, earthy, and spicy dishes.

Health Benefits: Though the aroma is not for everyone, I have experienced relief from tension and a considerable uplift. This strain can provide relief from depression, insomnia, nausea, pain, and stress. A couple of years ago I had knee surgery. This strain was an important part of my pain relief regimen.

DURBAN POISON

100% SATIVA

This sativa hails from South Africa and has gained notoriety around the world. It produces a stimulating, clear-focused, and energetic high, making it ideal for daytime use, as it promotes activity and productivity. Fans describe the experience as clear, bright, energetic, and promoting creativity. Ummm . . . yes, please!

THC: 15%–20%

CBD: 0.01%–0.02%

Flavor Profile: Earthy, sweet, and piney. This strain has a sweet anise taste and works well in warm spiced desserts like gingerbread, molasses cookies, and mulled cider.

Health Benefits: This strain offers relief from depression, ADHD, fatigue, headaches, migraines, and stress. A great strain for focus, it renders users clear minded and comes on superfast. When I am focused on writing, this is one of my go-to strains. This strain contains a good deal of THCV, a cannabinoid that is responsible for the euphoria and focus, leaving the user high functioning and raring to go. A daytime strain for sure.

FIRE OG

70% INDICA / 30% SATIVA

Commonly regarded to be the most powerful OG Kush strain on the planet, Fire OG is not recommended for inexperienced users. While most stick to very low doses, those partaking will experience instant cerebral stimulation leading to creative juices and waves of euphoria. Next comes the potent and relaxing body high, sending many to the couch or bed. Those with lower tolerances experience effects for up to three hours.

THC: 20%–28%

CBD: 0.36%–0.40%

Flavor Profile: A strain with the aroma of astringent lemon cleaning products (that really sounds worse than it is) with the taste of citrus, pine, and fuel. Thankfully the fuel taste is not particularly prominent, though there are hints of it on occasion. What's a fire without the fuel?

Health Benefits: Users of this strain find relief from anxiety disorders, depression, insomnia, nausea, pain, and a lack of appetite. The high is extremely potent, and I would suggest first-time users be cautious. A friend who is currently going through chemo is finding the strain helpful with her nausea and lack of appetite.

GELATO
50% INDICA / 50% SATIVA

This split hybrid was designed from a line of Thin Mint Girl Scout Cookies (GSC) and the fruity indica Sunset Sherbet. This strain has a great flavor profile with visual appeal. Fiery orange pistils stand against forest green leaves spotted with shades of dark purple. Although its high THC concentration leads to heavy effects of euphoria, many experience creativity, allowing users to remain uplifted and productive. Many turn to Gelato in social settings. Apparently this strain is also called "Larry Bird Kush," so that's a thing.

THC: 13%–25%

CBD: 0.1%–0.2%

Flavor Profile: A sweet and earthy aroma with mint and lavender, this strain's profile also produces a pungent citrus aroma. When grown correctly, the smoke is smooth and soft, never harsh. The aroma is powerful and distinctive, and you are not going to get away with taking a hit and expecting no one to notice! This strain pairs well with minty dishes such as a lemon-mint gelato.

Health Benefits: This fast-hitting strain helps ease anxiety, depression, insomnia, nausea, and pain. The uplifting effects have been helpful with folks suffering from PTSD, and, because the high is not terribly cerebral, you should not have issues with paranoia or other discomfort.

GIRL SCOUT COOKIES (GSC)

60% INDICA / 40% SATIVA

Taking several Cannabis Cups, this indica-dominant hybrid is a blend of two extremely popular strains on this list: OG Kush and Durban Poison. Fans find this strain produces a mellowing, therapeutic high and works well for both considerable relaxation and creating a mood for socializing.

THC: 18%–28%

CBD: 0.09%–0.2%

Flavor Profile: Both dark and skunky with notes of sweet sherbet atop fruity berry, orange, and lemon flavors. This strain is definitely a mix of both worlds, combining lemon, sweet, menthol, and diesel. It infuses well into desserts, which is not always an easy task.

Health Benefits: GSC is a powerful strain with benefits that are considerable. Expect relief from anxiety, arthritis, headaches, inflammation, lack of appetite, migraines, multiple sclerosis, nausea, pain, Parkinson's disease, PTSD, sleep disorders, spinal cord injury, and stress.

GODFATHER OG

60% INDICA / 40% SATIVA

This potent, sedating indica will be sure to reduce your stress and keep you in a deep relaxation throughout your medicating session. This bud is an offspring of XXX OG and Alpha OG and packs a punch with THC levels measuring as high as 28 percent. If a comfortable sleep is calling, look no further than the earthly toned Godfather OG.

THC: 25%–28%

CBD: 0.5%

Flavor Profile: This strain has strong scents of pine and earth, with hints of grape popping through, a rustic-tasting smoke, and a terrific high. We recommend pairing this strain with Italian dishes, obviously.

Health Benefits: This popular, award-winning strain starts off with a cerebral rush and gradually becomes the best of both worlds. The strain is good for both focus and relaxation, and that is a winning combo. Ease from depression, headaches, insomnia, and pain can be expected.

GORILLA GLUE #4

65% SATIVA / 35% INDICA

Also known as Original Gorilla Glue and GG4 for short, this heavy-handed hybrid is no longer a secret. GG4 took first place in multiple cannabis competitions. The strain got its name from both the sticky resin that collects on scissors when trimming, and its undeniable ability to leave users "glued" to the couch. Expect a full-body melt, despite its sativa dominance, accompanied by a straight-to-the-head buzz.

THC: 25%–32%

CBD: 0.05%–0.1%

Flavor Profile: Earthy, pungent, grassy, and sour, this is an anytime strain that is extremely resinous. It actually gives your mouth a kind of sticky feel. Not always an easy strain to pair with a lot of dishes, but we like to use it in dishes with dill, such as chicken noodle soup, egg salad, and potato salad.

Health Benefits: This strain offers significant relief from pain associated with muscle issues, including cramps and spasms. Relaxation can be expected, and it helps with insomnia. Additionally, you can expect relief from both nausea and lack of appetite.

GREEN CRACK

65% SATIVA / 35% INDICA

Rumor has it that this sativa was originally called Cush, yes with a C, but after rapper Snoop Dogg experienced its energizing and uplifting effects, he renamed it Green Crack. I'm not sure if that story is true, but I like it. This sativa produces an invigorating, joyful, and focused high, making it a good choice for daytime use. Patients dealing with stress, depression, or fatigue may find this an excellent remedy.

THC: 15%–25%

CBD: 0.0%–0.15%

Flavor Profile: Bright and citrusy, Green Crack is a blend of aromas: citrusy lemon and orange and earthy pine, but still tropical and spicy. I love this in savory dishes accented with lemon juice, like chicken piccata, lemon rosemary salmon, and hummus.

Health Benefits: This strain offers relief from anxiety, depression, fatigue, migraines, nausea, pain, PTSD, and stress. A couple of years ago, I did an event with veterans, many experiencing PTSD. This was one of the strains that seemed to offer serious relief.

JACK HERER

55% SATIVA / 45% INDICA

One of the most award-winning strains in cannabis history, Jack Herer is the namesake of a very influential cannabis activist who fought for the decriminalization of cannabis and expanded use of hemp. This classic sativa provides a clear-headed, creative, and motivating high, making it a great choice for daytime use. It tends to have a lot of varied phenotypes between growers and harvest, but most people experience it as the ideal "activity" strain.

THC: 18%–23%

CBD: 0.01%–0.2%

Flavor Profile: Jack Herer is one of my favorite strains. The taste is fruity, piney, skunky, and somewhat spicy. It's a very popular strain that can have a considerable taste variance with some of the flavors overshadowing others. This is a great strain for savory dishes. Think rosemary-roasted potatoes, mushroom risotto, and cedar-plank salmon.

Health Benefits: This strain offers relief from anxiety, arthritis, depression, fatigue, fibromyalgia, lack of focus, migraines, nausea, pain, and stress. You can expect a clear-headed ability to focus and get stuff done.

LAVENDER

80% INDICA / 20% SATIVA

This tasty indica-dominant hybrid from Soma Seeds tends to develop a beautiful purple hue. Its lineage, including the strain Afghani, lends a smooth but spicy, hash-like taste, while its Hawaiian lineage passes on a sweeter floral aroma. This beautiful bud is a well-balanced hybrid for a lazy, happy high.

THC: 19%

CBD: 1%

Flavor Profile: A spicy and floral aroma with a similar flavor, tasting of dried lavender, and a lovely sweetness that works beautifully with this peaceful high. Definitely use this strain to infuse dishes with cinnamon, coriander, or lavender.

Health Benefits: This strain offers a delightful, soothing, lazy high. Patients with ADHD, anorexia, anxiety, depression, insomnia, obsessive compulsive disorder, nausea, pain, and PTSD have found benefits and relief from this lovely strain.

NORTHERN LIGHTS

95% INDICA / 5% SATIVA

This well-known indica strain is the parent of many award-winners and a standout in its own right. Northern Lights produces a powerful body high and a relaxing sense of euphoria, like what you might feel when you first see the aurora borealis in all its glory. This great-tasting bud is a wonderful strain to have around for a relaxing, lazy day indoors.

THC: 16%–23%

CBD: 0.0%–0.01%

Flavor Profile: This tasty strain has both an earthy, piney taste with some sweet citrus notes. It has a good combination of flavors that work well together. I honestly would use this to infuse just about anything.

Health Benefits: With an impressive combination of health benefits, this is a good choice for people with anxiety disorder, arthritis, cachexia, depression, migraines, nausea, pain relief, and stress.

OG KUSH

55% SATIVA / 45% INDICA

This popular medical strain is extremely potent. There is some debate about what the "OG" stands for; some say "Ocean Grown" due to its California origins, while others say "Original Gangster," which is another cannabis strain. Regardless of its origins, this well-known, popular strain is one of the most common hybrids on the market.

THC: 20%–25%

CBD: 0.0%–0.5%

Flavor Profile: A winning combination of flavors, you will notice a combination of earthiness, pine, citrus, lemon, spice, wood, and oak. Someone described its scent as "old man cologne," and that nearly killed me. If you are having a cookout, use this strain in your marinade.

Health Benefits: A plethora of benefits, this strain is suggested for use by folks struggling with Alzheimer's disease, anxiety, arthritis, depression, fibromyalgia, glaucoma, headaches, migraines, multiple sclerosis, pain, PMS, PTSD, seizures, and stress.

PINEAPPLE EXPRESS

60% SATIVA / 40% INDICA

This descendant of potent and well-loved parent strains, Trainwreck and Hawaiian, Pineapple Express has a characteristic aroma likened to fresh apple and mango. Due to its sativa dominance, this hard-hitter will give users an energetic buzz leading to creative spurts and uplifted, relaxed effects. "Pineapple Express" is the unofficial term for a weather event that typically soaks the West Coast with moisture from Hawaii. And so, whenever a Pineapple Express is rolling through the Pacific Northwest, we must, must have this strain on hand while watching the movie *Pineapple Express*. Maybe even while eating a pineapple upside-down cake infused with Pineapple Express.

THC: 19%–27%

CBD: 0.1%–0.4%

Flavor Profile: This strain has a strong floral and tropical aroma, reminiscent of the strain's name. There are undertones of spice and cedar. This is a great strain to use in Thai dishes like mango and sticky rice or a spicy stir-fry with Thai basil and mango.

Health Benefits: Look for relief from anxiety, chronic stress, depression, fatigue, generalized restlessness, inflammation, migraines, muscle tightness, and pain. I generally love this strain, though there have been a couple of high-paranoia moments.

SOUR DIESEL (SOUR D)

SATIVA 70% / INDICA 30%

This terpene-rich sativa starts with an energizing buzz but also produces some intense cerebral effects. It is super pungent with an almost unrelenting skunky, lemon scent. Although classified as sativa, Sour Diesel can tend to give indica-ish effects, like couch lock and sedation. Its combination of effects makes it a versatile, interesting choice worth trying.

THC: 19%–25%

CBD: 0.2%–0.5%

Flavor Profile: As its name alludes, expect a diesel, earthy, and pungent flavor. I have a bunch of friends who absolutely loathe this taste and others who find it is their jam. I think it's the same friends who like a peaty scotch.

Health Benefits: Users of this strain find relief from depression, fatigue, nausea, pain, and stress. A friend who has bipolar disorder says that he can get positive results during his down periods.

STRAWBERRY COUGH

85% SATIVA / 15% INDICA

This lovely sativa produces uplifting, euphoric effects. Something in this strain tends to make people cough when they smoke it, hence the name (oh yeah, and it smells like lovely strawberries). This joyous strain is buzzy, promotes creativity, and is relaxing. Grab this strain when you need to meet some deadlines with a smile on your face.

THC: 13%–23%

CBD: 0.1%–0.2%

Flavor Profile: This strain is largely reminiscent of strawberries. It is both sweet and a bit skunky. It does cause a considerable amount of dry mouth when smoked, so suck on something!

Health Benefits: This exceptional strain is one of my favorites, offering relief from significant anxiety and sleep issues. It seems to allay stress for hours, allowing me to resume normal activities. In addition, it can treat migraines, PTSD, anxiety disorders, and stress while stimulating appetite.

WHITE WIDOW

60% SATIVA / 40% INDICA

White Widow brings on a potent high that can produce both paranoia and lethargy, so it may not be for everyone. This resin-coated strain can appear white, hence the name. White Widow will leave users with a powerful euphoria and energy, which is great for stimulating conversation, listening to music, and engaging in creative tasks. If you have a tendency toward paranoia with some strains, skip this one.

THC: 18%–25%

CBD: 0.0%–0.05%

Flavor Profile: Sweet and floral notes with earthy, woody, and spicy undertones. I'd use this strain to infuse simple foods like granola, bread, or a nut mix.

Health Benefits: Patients can find considerable ease from anxiety, depression, migraines, nausea, pain, PMS, sleep disorders, and stress from this resinous strain.

CANNA-BUTTER,
PAGE 43

CHAPTER 3

Cooking with Cannabis

With a few simple tips, you too can be a master in the art of cooking with cannabis. You'll learn how to use fancy words like "decarboxylation" and "infusion calibration" to really impress your friends. But more important, you will be able to craft cannabis edibles that will be expertly dosed to meet your needs and expectations. This is not a chapter to skip—this is where it all begins.

EQUIPPING YOUR CANNABIS KITCHEN

There is not a whole lot of equipment you need to make your own infusions, though some pieces of equipment will make it easier and give you more exact results. A scale and a grinder are helpful and a double boiler makes infusion easy, but if you have a metal bowl that fits on top of a pot, that will work fine, too. Have cheesecloth for straining or a very fine mesh strainer. If you have both, you can lay the cheesecloth in the fine mesh strainer, and your oil will be free of any debris.

Here's a list of a few kitchen items we find helpful for making cannabis infusions:

Cheesecloth: This loose-woven cloth is a handy tool for straining infusions and allows for easy cleanup.

Digital scale: When measuring cannabis, digital scales are an absolute necessity if you care at all about accuracy. Look for one that will measure in 0.1-gram increments.

Double boiler: A double boiler is basically one pot that fits into another, or a metal bowl sitting over a pot. The bottom pot is filled with water and the top pot (or bowl) is filled with the ingredients that shouldn't receive direct heat, like chocolate. Do not let the bowl or inner pan touch the water below, and do not let the pan run out of water.

Fine mesh strainer: A fine mesh strainer will pay for itself, I promise. Look for one that will securely sit on top of a bowl to allow for easy, hands-free straining.

Food processor: For chopping up your cannabis, a food processor can really make a difference.

Slow cooker: Another popular method of infusion is the slow cooker. A slow cooker on low or high is a gentle way to infuse oil or butter. I find that 160°F for 4 to 6 hours makes a terrific infusion.

Rules of the Road in Cannabis Cookery

1. **LABEL EVERYTHING.** This is critical. No one should ever eat an infused food without their knowledge. I've personally never had it happen, but I can imagine that it would be terrifying.
2. **DON'T EVER GIVE CANNABIS EDIBLES TO KIDS.** Keep them out of the reach of children. Never leave cannabis or cannabis edibles on a kitchen counter or a bedside table or easily accessible in the refrigerator. Everyone's busy and it's easy to forget. Don't forget.
3. **DON'T EVER GIVE CANNABIS EDIBLES TO PETS.** No. It's not funny.

SHOPPING FOR CANNABIS

States that have legalized cannabis, either recreational or medicinal, sell products in a variety of forms in licensed shops called dispensaries. These dispensaries sell tested cannabis, allowing you to know the precise potency of what's available.

When purchasing cannabis to use in an infusion, research flavor profiles and strain effects so that you find something that will give you a smell and terpene profile that works for you. We recommend letting your nose guide you to the most pleasing strain. As you become more familiar with various strains, you'll start to zero in on what you like. Personally, we like to smoke a bowl or a joint of the particular strain we want to use. You can often buy a pre-roll or gram to do a taste/effects test.

If you have a dispensary that sells trim of the plant, or know a grower, that is an economical way to infuse. We often infuse with trim or shake at considerably lower prices and still get fine results—even at just about half the potency of using cannabis buds.

Cannabis is best stored in cool, dark places to maintain its cannabinoid profile. Mason jars that will keep the cannabis airtight are a great choice. The ideal temperature for storing cannabis is 70°F. Although you may not be able to get that number exactly, a dark cabinet will work well. Cannabis, if treated right, will keep for several months (or even over a year for infusion purposes, though it might be too dry to smoke) as long as you limit exposure to light, moisture, and heat.

DECARBOXYLATION

As mentioned in the first chapter, if you are looking to get the highest potency out of your edibles, you must decarboxylate the cannabis before you infuse your oil or butter. When you smoke cannabis, the decarb process happens when you light up. For cooking purposes, you need to convert all the cannabinoid THCA, which is non-psychoactive, to THC, the cannabinoid we know and love for the experience of being "high."

The decarb process works best when the oven temperature is 240°F, and the baking time that seems to fully decarb the flower is 40 minutes. At a low temperature, you are preserving most terpenes, the essential oils in the cannabis plant that inform the flavor profiles of the cannabis, but more important, you are also preserving considerable health benefits.

At Laurie + MaryJane, we constantly test our infusions for potency and cannabinoid profile retention. And our tests indicate that when we decarb before the infusion process, all the THCA is converted to THC. Without an initial decarb, often THCA is prominent in the cannabinoid profile of the infusion. And once you've made your infusion, it is difficult and time consuming to decarb the infusion any further. If you have the time (and it's only minutes), decarboxylate.

Storing Decarb'd Cannabis

Store decarboxylated cannabis in an airtight container in a cool, dark place. We like to vacuum seal the flower and keep it in the freezer for extended storage. If you are going to use it fairly soon, a Mason jar in a cool, dark place works well. Be aware that over time, with exposure to heat and light, THC and CBD will slowly degrade into CBN, which is very sedating. If you do not want the sedating effects of CBN, keep your flower stored properly. If you store it properly, you can use your decarb for at least a year.

Eating versus Smoking Cannabis

When you inhale cannabis, the burning of the flower activates THCA into THC, which is then absorbed into the bloodstream within minutes. When you eat anything infused with decarboxylated (activated from THCA to THC by heat) cannabis, THC is first digested in the stomach and then moves to the liver. From the liver it is metabolized and converted into a slightly different form of THC (11-hydroxy-delta-9-THC) that crosses the blood-brain barrier more easily and is thought to have more of a psychotropic effect and a greater degree of sedation and relaxation. If too much is consumed, it can result in nausea, dizziness, hallucinations, and severe anxiety. Once the liver converts the THC into delta-9 THC, it enters the bloodstream. Effects begin anywhere from 45 minutes to 3 hours after ingesting and can last several hours.

There are several factors that contribute to the wide time range for the effects' onset. Ingesting edibles on an empty stomach can bring on the effects faster than a full stomach, as can a faster metabolism. However, hard candies, gum, and tincture drops that are taken sublingually (under the tongue), and anything else absorbed in the mouth, will take effect almost immediately and wear off within two to three hours. The THC in drinks, chocolates, and some other edibles can also be absorbed in the mouth to some degree, depending on the length of time it's held in the mouth.

Like inhaling, ingesting cannabis can lead to a range of effects. While the effects can differ among people and strains, most people may feel relaxation, sedation, euphoria, anxiety, paranoia, verbosity, and/or increased appetite. It also causes physiological effects such as increased appetite (the "munchies"), rapid heart rate, dry mouth, and/or red eyes.

Decarboxylated Cannabis

PREP TIME: 5 MINUTES | COOK TIME: 40 MINUTES | YIELD: VARIABLE

If the odor of cannabis is problematic for you, put it in a turkey bag before setting it on the baking sheet. We do pounds at a time like this, and it's pretty awesome, almost entirely eliminating the smell.

Also, if you have a sous vide machine, decarbing your cannabis in a vacuum-sealed bag works beautifully, as does placing the cannabis in a sealed Mason jar in a slow cooker half filled with water. Burp the jar every half hour to be sure the pressure doesn't become too strong. If using the sous vide or slow cooker method, allow the plant material to decarb for 90 minutes.

Your desired amount of cannabis, buds or trim

1. Preheat the oven to 240°F.
2. With gloved hands, break apart any very large cannabis buds. On a rimmed baking sheet, spread out the cannabis.
3. Bake until the cannabis is lightly browned, about 40 minutes.
4. Let it cool fully, then pulse it in a food processor until coarsely ground.

EXTRACTIONS, TINCTURES, AND INFUSIONS

As you know by now, cooking with cannabis is not simply chopping up your bud and mixing it into a dish. It first involves extracting or infusing the cannabis into another material. Not just any material will do, either. Some of the most commonly used include butter, cooking oils, alcohol, and vegetable glycerin. We use cooking fats for our cannabis infusions, as fat is particularly good at extracting the full spectrum of cannabinoids and terpenes. The plant's resin is fully soluble in fats and blends nicely for a homogenous infusion. We find cooking oil and butter infusions are the most versatile and reliable in the kitchen when making edibles.

While you will find that all the recipes in this book use infused oil or butter, tinctures are another popular method of infusion, typically using either alcohol or vegetable glycerin. For tinctures, you can add your decarb'd cannabis (unless you want THCA or CBDA) to a jar with alcohol or vegetable glycerin and wait a few months, shaking every so often. It can be fun to make a tincture with cooking brandy or rum and spice up your dishes. Vegetable glycerin is also water-soluble, making it a great option to add to beverages.

What to Do If You've Had Too Much

Too much THC can be a very unpleasant thing. And it happens at least once to pretty much everyone who is learning to cook with a cannabis infusion of oil or butter. Tasting throughout the day, or one bite too many can add up to too much, creating a miserable, though non-life-threatening, situation. It can cause dizziness, nausea/vomiting, hallucinations, poor motor skills, and extreme anxiety—not fun. Just remember that it is not fatal, and it will go away in time. When it comes to cannabis, less is surely more. While you wait for symptoms to go away, try to remain calm and do not drive or operate heavy machinery. Take it slow, and if it goes sideways:

- sleep
- drink a lot of water
- watch a Disney movie (not *Bambi*)
- take some CBD
- eat an orange
- remember that you will be fine
- chew a tiny bit of black peppercorn to tamp down anxiety
- listen to music
- color
- eat something not infused

Canna-Butter

PREP TIME: 15 MINUTES | COOK TIME: 3 HOURS | YIELD: 2 CUPS

Follow the directions and you will make the best butter your cannabis will allow. The truth is that the canna-butter is only as good and strong as the ingredients you make it with. Bear in mind that the stronger the cannabis, the stronger the butter, so plan accordingly.

1 pound (4 sticks) unsalted butter

7 grams cannabis, decarboxylated (page 38) and coarsely ground

STOVETOP

1. In a medium saucepan, bring 1 quart of water to a boil. You can vary the amount, just be sure that the marijuana is always floating about 1½ to 2 inches from the bottom of the pan.

2. Add the butter to the boiling water and allow it to melt completely.

3. Once the butter has melted, reduce the heat to a gentle simmer and add the cannabis. Cover to reduce the smell, if desired. Cook for around 3 hours, stirring occasionally. You can tell it's done when the top of the mixture looks dark, glossy, and thick.

OVEN

1. Preheat the oven to 220°F.

2. Place the butter and cannabis in an oven-safe saucepan. Add 1 quart of water.

3. Cover and place in the oven for 3 hours, stirring occasionally. You can tell it's done when the top of the mixture turns from really watery to glossy and thick.

TO FINISH

1. While the canna-butter is cooking, set up a bowl to hold the finished product. There are a couple of ways to do the straining. I like to use a deep heatproof glass bowl and a fine mesh strainer lined with cheesecloth. You can also tie a double layer of cheesecloth around a large heatproof bowl with twine, making it taut across the top.

continued

2. Strain the canna-butter into the bowl, taking care not to spill any. When the saucepan is empty, carefully pick up the cheesecloth from all four sides and, wearing gloves or using clean hands, squeeze out all of the remaining butter from the cannabis.

3. Allow the canna-butter to cool at room temperature for about an hour. Place in the refrigerator until the butter has solidified and separated from the water. The THC and other properties have attached to the butter, and you are just about there.

4. Run a knife around the edge and lift the butter off the water. Place it upside down on your work surface and scrape off any of the cooking water. Your canna-butter is ready to roll. Label and store it in an airtight container in the refrigerator for up to 1 month or 6 months in the freezer. To freeze, use a vacuum-sealed bag or wrap well in aluminum foil or parchment paper, then seal in a freezer storage bag or airtight container.

Canna-Coconut Oil

PREP TIME: 15 MINUTES | COOK TIME: 3 HOURS | YIELD: 2 CUPS

Canna-coconut oil does double-duty as a cooking oil/ingredient and a topical pain reliever. I add it to smoothies and use it to cook curries and vegetables, as well as using it as a massage oil.

2 cups (16 ounces) coconut oil

7 grams cannabis, decarboxylated (page 38) and coarsely ground

STOVETOP

1. In a medium saucepan, bring a quart of water to a boil. You can vary the amounts, just be sure that the marijuana is always floating about 1½ to 2 inches from the bottom of the pan.

2. When the water is boiling, place the coconut oil in the saucepan and allow it to melt completely.

3. Once the oil has melted, turn down the heat to a gentle simmer and add the cannabis. Cover to reduce the smell, if desired.

4. Cook for around 3 hours, stirring occasionally. You can tell it's done when the top of the mixture turns from really watery to glossy and thick.

OVEN

1. Preheat the oven to 220°F.

2. Place oil and cannabis in an oven-safe saucepan. Add 1 quart of water.

3. Cover and place in the oven for 3 hours, stirring occasionally. You can tell it's done when the top of the mixture turns from really watery to glossy and thick.

TO FINISH

1. While the canna-coconut oil is cooking, set up a bowl to hold the finished product. There are a couple of ways to do the straining. I like to use a deep heatproof glass bowl and a fine mesh strainer lined with cheesecloth. You can also tie a double layer of cheesecloth around a large heatproof bowl with twine, making it taut across the top.

continued

Canna-Coconut Oil, *continued*

2. Strain the canna-coconut oil into the bowl, taking care not to spill any. When the saucepan is empty, carefully pick up the cheesecloth from all four sides and, wearing gloves or using clean hands, squeeze out all of the remaining butter.

3. Allow the canna-coconut oil to cool at room temperature for about an hour. Place in the refrigerator until the oil has solidified and separated from the water. The THC and other properties have attached to the oil, and you are just about there.

4. Run a knife around the edge and lift the solidified oil off the water. Place upside down on your work surface and scrape off any of the cooking water. Your canna-coconut oil is ready to roll. Label and store in the refrigerator in an airtight container for up to a month or freeze for up to 6 months. To freeze, use a vacuum-sealed bag or wrap well in aluminum foil or parchment paper, then seal in a freezer storage bag or airtight container.

Using Your Slow Cooker for Infusing

There are lots of folks who make their cannabis infusions in a slow cooker. It's a good technique, but just be sure that your cooker has a low enough setting; even on the Low setting some slow cookers are still too hot for these infusions. Use a thermometer to make sure your infusion stays in the 200° to 240°F range. That said, if you are making canna-butter or canna-coconut oil, you can use the water method, and you won't have to worry. The beauty of a slow cooker is that the temperature should be maintained throughout the cooking process. Cook your canna-butter or oil in your slow cooker (at 200° to 240°F) for 3 hours after decarboxylation.

Canna-Oil

PREP TIME: 15 MINUTES | COOK TIME: 3 HOURS | YIELD: 2 CUPS

Infusing cooking oil requires a technique different from the one used for butter and coconut oil. Butter and coconut oil solidify when chilled, causing it to separate from the water it is cooked in. Oils like canola and olive oil thicken but don't totally solidify when chilled, so another method is needed, namely direct infusion into the oil, with no added water. The finished oil will have a green tinge because of the cannabis, and a cannabis taste. As with Canna-Butter and Canna-Coconut Oil, you can do this on a stovetop or in the oven.

2 cups cooking oil of your choice (olive, avocado, grapeseed, sunflower, canola, or a mixture)

7 grams cannabis, decarboxylated (page 38) and coarsely ground

STOVETOP

1. In a large saucepan, slowly heat the oil over low heat. You want the temperature of the oil to stay between 200 to 240°F.
2. Whisk in the cannabis. Cover with a lid to reduce the smell, if desired. Cook for 3 hours, stirring occasionally.

OVEN

1. Preheat the oven to 220°F.
2. In a large oven-safe saucepan, whisk together the oil and cannabis. Cover and place in the oven. Cook for 3 hours, stirring occasionally.

TO FINISH

1. Whether on stovetop or in the oven, cook for 3 hours, stirring every 30 minutes. Occasional bubbles in the mixture are okay, but do not let it boil.
2. After 3 hours, remove the oil from the heat or the oven and allow it to cool slightly (hot oil can be dangerous to handle).
3. While the oil cools, line a strainer or sieve with cheesecloth and place it over a large glass bowl.
4. Pour the cooled oil through the cheesecloth into the bowl. Press down on the cannabis with a spatula to extract all the oil. Discard the cheesecloth.

continued

5. Transfer the oil to a glass jar with a lid and store it in a cool, dark place for up to 6 months.

Tip: Cannabis-infused olive oil is terrific to have on hand. Where do we begin? Pasta, vegetables, all kinds of fish, poultry, and wonderful desserts all benefit. Place it in a spouted jar and add a cannabis-infused drizzle to everything from soup to fresh berries.

Freezing Canna-Butter and Canna-Oils for Easy Use

Whenever we make an infusion, we pour the infused oil or butter into ice cube trays, and once solid, place them in resealable plastic freezer bags, label them, and store them in the freezer. Prominently. We can't stress enough that you need to label everything containing cannabis. If you need to be discreet, label them cod liver oil. That seems to be a pretty universal turn-off.

DOSING

With a few adjustments, anything can be infused. And with a little basic math, you can know the potency and adjust it to your desired dose. If you start by making canna-butter or canna-coconut oil as outlined in this book, ½ teaspoon is used to make 1 serving. For the purposes of this book, we consider one serving to be 5mg THC. If you want to adjust the amount of THC in your serving, adjust the ratio of cannabis flower to butter/oil.

Once you've added in the appropriate amount of canna-butter or canna-oil, you may need to adjust the flavors to cover the cannabis taste. If your recipe is already a flavorful dish, you may not need any adjustments. However, if it is more subtle, you will need to increase the flavorful ingredient(s) and/or add flavors such as chocolate, coffee, peanut butter, and cinnamon.

The most important part of making edibles is the calculation of THC/CBD per serving. And to know how to calculate the THC/CBD per serving, you will need to know the potency of your infusion. And to know the potency of your infusion, you will need to know the potency of your cannabis. In our kitchen, we cook with 20 percent THC cannabis. The cannabis you cook with, in all likelihood is very different. Perhaps stronger, perhaps weaker. Either way, if you want a 10mg THC per teaspoon dose, you'll have to make some adjustments. It involves a little math, but nothing you can't handle. In fact, we've made it even easier for you with the chart in the next section on calculating your dosage (page 51). Infused butter and oil can be very potent, so be careful when ingesting until you know your dosage and the potency of your infusion.

During the decarboxylation and infusion process, there is going to be some loss of THC/CBD. But if you follow our guide, it will be minimal. We've found our butter and oil infusions to have about a 20 percent loss of THC. So, 1 gram of 20 percent THC cannabis has 200mg THC, but infused into butter or oil, you will get about 160mg THC. The biggest key to maintaining potency is to extract at a low temperature.

Finding Your THC Sweet Spot

Our edibles motto is "start low and go slow." The recipes in this book have a serving size of 5mg THC. Although this is a general suggestion for cannabis consumption, when starting out making your own edibles, we advise starting with a smaller dose. We actually know quite a few people whose comfortable dose is under 2mg THC. We recommend being at home for the evening and trying a small dose, something between 2mg and 5mg THC. Do not have any more that day so you can have a clear view of how it affects you. If you find it wasn't enough of the experience you are seeking, the next day double that first dose. Wait, and do the same thing each day until you find your comfort zone. Once you know your ideal potency, you can use the chart opposite to determine the proper amount of cannabis to use in your infusions.

HOW TO CALCULATE DOSING

Our infusions are calibrated to produce 10mg THC per teaspoon using cannabis with 20 percent THC. If you have cannabis with a different percentage, use the table below to determine the amount of cannabis to use in your infusion.

For 2 cups (16 ounces) of infused cooking oil or butter, use the chart below to determine how much cannabis you want to add to your infusion to produce the desired potency per teaspoon.

POTENCY PER TEASPOON OF INFUSION (MG THC)

THC % OF CANNABIS FLOWER

CANNABIS FLOWER USED IN INFUSION (GRAMS)	5%	10%	15%	20%	25%	30%
5	2.1	4.2	6.3	8.3	10.4	12.5
7.5	3.1	6.3	9.4	12.5	15.6	18.8
10	4.2	8.3	12.5	16.7	20.8	25
12.5	5.2	10.4	15.6	20.8	26	31.3
15	6.3	12.5	18.8	25	31.3	37.5
17.5	7.3	14.6	21.9	29.2	36.5	43.8
20	8.3	16.7	25	33.3	41.7	50
22.5	9.4	18.8	28.1	37.5	46.9	56.3
25	10.4	20.8	31.3	41.7	52.1	62.5

If you don't know the THC content of your cannabis, follow our main infusion guide and try a quarter teaspoon to assess your reaction to its potency. Wait a day to assess its effect and take notes on how to dose that infusion going forward.

PART

2

THE RECIPES

GARLIC-PARMESAN
POTCORN, PAGE 57

CHAPTER 4

Marvelous Munchies

I am an hors d'oeuvres lover. I have been known to camp out near the kitchen at catered events to get first dibs on what's coming out. I make friends with the servers, and sometimes they will seek me out. I love that. Infusing individual bites makes dosing easy and removes any guesswork. If you intend to make munchies a part of your meal, you probably should not infuse anything else. Don't overdo it—too much cannabis is not pleasant. The right amount of cannabis . . . priceless!

Classic Deviled Eggs

PREP TIME: 35 MINUTES | COOK TIME: 15 MINUTES | YIELD: 6 SERVINGS (2 EGG HALVES PER SERVING)
THC: 5MG PER SERVING (2.5MG PER EGG HALF) | GLUTEN-FREE | NUT-FREE | VEGETARIAN

I think deviled eggs might be a love-hate food for a lot of people. Personally, I've never tasted a deviled egg I didn't like. I've had them stuffed with all kinds of things, including smoked salmon and recently tapenade and feta. Tasty, but I missed this yolk filling.

6 large eggs, hardboiled, peeled, and halved

2 tablespoons mayonnaise

1 tablespoon Canna-Butter (page 43), melted and cooled

1 to 2 tablespoons sweet pickle relish

1 teaspoon finely minced shallot

1 teaspoon Dijon mustard

Salt

Coarsely ground black pepper

Smoked paprika, for dusting

1. Place the eggs on your work surface. Gently remove the yolks and place them in a medium bowl. Set the whites aside on a large plate. To the bowl, add the mayonnaise, canna-butter, relish, shallot, and mustard, and mash everything together until smooth. Season with salt and pepper.

2. Carefully fill the cavities of the egg whites with the yolk mixture. Sprinkle with the paprika.

Storage: Once stuffed, you have a day, maybe two to consume them. If you must, cover them with plastic wrap as tightly as possible and refrigerate. If you have a bunch, sandwich them together and wrap well. You can also mash the stuffed eggs and make a rad deviled egg salad sandwich. Add lettuce and tomato and spread the bread with a little Dijon mustard.

The Perfect Hardboiled Egg

Place the eggs in a single layer in a saucepan and cover with 2 inches of water. Bring to a boil, cover, turn the heat to low, and boil an additional minute. Remove from the heat and leave covered for 15 minutes. Place the eggs in a bowl of ice water for 10 minutes. Crack the shells and peel the eggs under cold running water. Dry them on a clean dish towel.

Garlic-Parmesan Potcorn

PREP TIME: 35 MINUTES | COOK TIME: 15 MINUTES | YIELD: 9 SERVINGS (1 CUP PER SERVING)

THC: 5MG PER SERVING | GLUTEN-FREE | NUT-FREE | VEGETARIAN

Infused popcorn is a great snack. In order to keep the dosing legit, do like they do in the movie theatres and drizzle the infused butter on top. If you don't want to pop the kernels yourself, look for plain popcorn at your local market. Don't get the kind that's already cheesy. The popcorn tastes better and has a better texture when it's plain. If you want to go with a sweet flavor profile, add 2 tablespoons sugar and 1 teaspoon of cinnamon to the melted butters. Yum.

5 tablespoons popcorn kernels (about 9 cups popped)

4½ tablespoons unsalted butter, melted

1½ tablespoons Canna-Butter (page 43), melted

¼ cup chopped fresh Italian parsley

½ teaspoon garlic powder

½ teaspoon kosher salt

¼ teaspoon coarse ground black pepper

½ cup grated Parmesan cheese

1. Pop the popcorn according to the package directions. Set aside the popped corn in a large bowl.
2. Over low heat, in a small saucepan, melt the butters. Once melted, turn off the heat and stir in the parsley, garlic powder, salt, and pepper.
3. Divide the popcorn into 9 (1-cup) portions in cups or bowls with enough room to shake a bit to mix the popcorn and topping. Spoon an equal amount of the butter mixture over each bowl and mix. Sprinkle each with the Parmesan cheese.

Storage: For your leftover popcorn, use sandwich-size storage bags to separate each serving. Enjoy within 2 to 3 days.

Cheesy Sausage-Stuffed Mushrooms

PREP TIME: 20 MINUTES | COOK TIME: 40 MINUTES | YIELD: 8 SERVINGS (2 MUSHROOMS PER SERVING)

THC: 5MG PER SERVING (2.5MG PER MUSHROOM) | NUT-FREE

16 extra-large white button mushrooms

2 tablespoons extra-virgin olive oil

½ cup chopped scallions, both green and white parts

2 garlic cloves, minced

12 ounces ground spicy sausage

⅔ cup dry Italian breadcrumbs

4 ounces cream cheese, at room temperature

⅓ cup grated Romano cheese

4 teaspoons Canna-Butter (page 43) or Canna-Oil (page 47), at room temperature

Salt

Freshly ground black pepper

1. Preheat the oven to 325°F.

2. Clean the mushrooms using a damp paper towel to remove any dirt. Do not run under water. Remove and finely chop the stems and set aside.

3. In a medium saucepan, heat the olive oil over low heat. Add the scallions, garlic, and chopped mushroom stems and cook until tender, 5 to 7 minutes. Add the sausage, increase the heat to medium, and cook, stirring a few times, until cooked through, about another 10 minutes. Remove from the heat.

4. In a large bowl, combine the sausage mixture with the breadcrumbs, cream cheese, Romano cheese, and canna-butter. Sprinkle with salt and pepper.

5. Place the mushroom caps on a rimmed baking sheet. Scoop a heaping tablespoon of the filling into each of the mushrooms.

6. Bake the mushrooms until the cheese is melted and the mushrooms turn golden brown, about 25 minutes.

Storage: Keep the mushrooms in an airtight container in the refrigerator for 4 to 5 days. Reheat in the microwave for 1 to 2 minutes on medium power. They won't be crisp, but they will be tasty.

Beef Sliders with The Works

PREP TIME: 10 MINUTES | COOK TIME: 10 MINUTES | YIELD: 6 SERVINGS (1 SLIDER PER SERVING)

THC: 5MG PER SLIDER | NUT-FREE

Sliders rock. If they are on a menu, I'll order them—I can't resist baby burgers. I grew up near a White Castle, and just about every Sunday my dad would take my brother and me. He and I had contests about who could eat more burgers. I have a bit of shame, because I won, and wow, that was way too many burgers.

1 pound ground beef

1 teaspoon Dijon mustard

1 tablespoon Canna-Oil (page 47)

1 garlic clove, minced

½ teaspoon salt

¼ teaspoon freshly ground black pepper

¼ teaspoon smoked paprika

2 tablespoons canola oil

½ cup grated Cheddar cheese

6 slider buns

6 slices red onion

3 slices bacon, cooked till crisp and cut into 2-inch pieces

18 slices pickle

Mustard (optional)

Ketchup (optional)

1. In a medium bowl, gently but thoroughly mix the beef, mustard, canna-oil, garlic, salt, pepper, and paprika together. Form the meat into 6 patties of equal size.

2. In a large skillet, heat the canola oil over medium heat. Cook the burgers to your desired degree of doneness (3 to 4 minutes per side for medium-rare). When you flip the burgers, top each with an equal amount of the cheese.

3. When the burgers are done, place one on each of the buns. Top with the onion, bacon, and pickles. Top with mustard (if using) and ketchup (if using).

Storage: This is not a great leftover food. I don't know about you, but I have never had much success reheating burgers, including minis. However, since it's the burger meat that's infused, you can crumble the cooked meat into a salad or casserole and enjoy these in a whole new way.

Mini Grilled Cheese Bites

PREP TIME: 5 MINUTES | COOK TIME: 12 MINUTES | YIELD: 2 SERVINGS (4 BITES PER SERVING)

THC: 5MG PER SERVING | NUT-FREE | VEGETARIAN

The ultimate infused comfort food, these crunchy bites are fantastic on their own, or you can dip them in your favorite tomato sauce or soup. Vary the cheese to suit your preference—the choices are plentiful. If you are so inclined, cut each sandwich into 8 pieces and drop them in a creamy tomato soup.

4 slices sourdough bread

1 teaspoon Canna-Butter (page 43), softened

4 slices Cheddar cheese

4 slices Swiss cheese

2 slices Muenster cheese

Tomato slices (optional)

Grilled vegetables (optional)

Avocado slices (optional)

Jalapeño slices (optional)

1 tablespoon canola oil

1. Butter two of the bread slices with ½ teaspoon of canna-butter each. Top each buttered slice with two slices of Cheddar, two slices of Swiss, and one slice of Muenster. If using, add the tomatoes, grilled vegetables, avocado, and/or jalapeño. Close the sandwiches.

2. In a large nonstick skillet, heat the oil over medium heat, tilting the pan to coat the bottom with it. Add the sandwiches and cook until golden brown, 4 to 5 minutes. Flip the sandwiches over and cook until the other side is golden, 4 to 5 minutes longer.

3. Cut each sandwich into quarters and serve.

Storage: Grilled cheese is tough to save, if you even have leftovers. But it's not impossible; just wrap it tightly and refrigerate. To reheat, I would do a quick sauté in a pan rather than use a microwave, or you will lose the crispiness we all live for.

Pigs in a Blanket

PREP TIME: 10 MINUTES | COOK TIME: 17 MINUTES | YIELD: 12 SERVINGS (2 PIGS PER SERVING)

THC: 5MG PER SERVING (2.5MG PER PIG) | NUT-FREE

In the list of my 10 favorite foods, pigs in blankets are in the top five. Sometimes I stick a little cheese in the pastry before rolling it up, and that's a taste sensation. I make sure I keep my eye on the trays that circulate at cocktail parties, also taking two, one for a friend.

Nonstick baking spray

1 (8-ounce) package crescent roll dough

2 tablespoons Canna-Butter (page 43), melted and cooled

24 mini hot dogs

Ketchup, for serving

Mustard, for serving

Mayonnaise, for serving

1. Preheat the oven to 340°F. Coat a baking sheet with nonstick spray.
2. Unroll the dough and separate it into 8 triangles. Cut each triangle into 3 smaller triangles. Brush each triangle with the canna-butter. Place 1 hot dog on the shortest side of each triangle; roll up to the opposite point. Place the pigs in a blanket seam-side down on the prepared baking sheet. Repeat with the remaining dough and hot dogs.
3. Bake until deep golden brown, 15 to 17 minutes. Immediately remove from the baking sheet.
4. Serve with ketchup, mustard, and mayonnaise.

Storage: These little beauties can be stored in an airtight container in the refrigerator. Reheat in a 340°F oven for 5 to 7 minutes. Microwaving will leave them a bit soggy, but it will do the trick.

Feta-Spinach Phyllo Triangles

PREP TIME: 20 MINUTES | COOK TIME: 22 MINUTES | YIELD: 8 SERVINGS (2 TRIANGLES PER SERVING)

THC: 5MG PER SERVING (2.5MG PER TRIANGLE) | NUT-FREE | VEGETARIAN

Mini spanakopita bites are my jam. And it's pretty easy to convince myself that they are healthy. Check out all that spinach—it has to be. Phyllo dough is a wonderful thing to infuse with layer upon layer of buttery pastry. These are delicious with a simple dipping sauce, like yogurt whirred together with fresh mint in a blender until smooth or olive oil with red pepper flakes or another spice or seasoning blend.

5 tablespoons unsalted butter, divided

½ cup finely chopped onion

1 (10-ounce) package frozen chopped spinach, thawed, drained, and squeezed of all liquid

1 cup crumbled feta cheese

1 large egg, lightly beaten

Salt

Freshly ground black pepper

4 teaspoons Canna-Butter (page 43)

8 sheets defrosted phyllo dough

1. Preheat the oven to 340°F.

2. In a medium skillet, melt 1 tablespoon of unsalted butter over medium heat and cook the onion, stirring a few times, until softened, 5 to 7 minutes. Remove the skillet from the heat and stir in the spinach, feta, and egg. Mix well. Season with salt and pepper.

3. In a small skillet, melt the remaining 4 tablespoons butter with the canna-butter and mix well.

4. Lay out one layer of phyllo dough and brush with the melted butter from the small skillet. Top with another layer of phyllo and brush with the butter. Repeat with a third layer of phyllo. Using a sharp knife, cut the rectangle lengthwise into three even-size pieces.

5. Place a heaping tablespoon of the spinach mixture in the lower left corner of one of the pieces and fold up as you would a flag, folding the lower corner up to form a triangle and continuing to fold up into a triangle.

6. Place the triangles on a baking sheet and bake until golden brown and puffed, about 15 minutes.

Storage: Keep the phyllo triangles in an airtight container in the refrigerator for up to 5 days or freeze for up to 2 months. To freeze, place the uncooked triangles on a baking sheet and freeze, then transfer to an airtight container. Your only hope for a flaky leftover triangle is to reheat in a 340°F oven for 10 minutes if refrigerated or 15 to 20 minutes if frozen. If they begin to get too brown, cover them loosely with foil.

Spicy Chicken Canna-Quesadillas

PREP TIME: 20 MINUTES | COOK TIME: 22 MINUTES | YIELD: 4 SERVINGS (1 QUESADILLA PER SERVING)

THC: 5MG PER QUESADILLA | NUT-FREE

If you don't eat chicken, you can substitute tofu, shrimp, or beef. The spicing is robust, leaving no taste of cannabis—just a tantalizing mix of flavors and textures. If you use corn tortillas, you have a gluten-free option.

1¼ pounds boneless skinless chicken breasts, diced into ½-inch cubes

2 teaspoons chili powder

1 teaspoon ground cumin

¾ teaspoon salt

½ teaspoon freshly ground black pepper

2 teaspoons Canna-Butter (page 43)

4 tablespoons (½ stick) unsalted butter, divided

1 cup chopped bell pepper

⅔ cup chopped red onion

2 garlic cloves, minced

4 (10-inch) flour tortillas

1½ cups shredded Cheddar cheese

1½ cups shredded Monterey Jack cheese

4 lime wedges

Guacamole, for serving (optional)

Sour cream, for serving (optional)

Pico de gallo or salsa, for serving (optional)

1. In a large bowl, combine the chicken, chili powder, cumin, salt, and pepper. Allow to sit, covered, for 30 minutes in the refrigerator.

2. In a large skillet, heat the canna-butter and 1 tablespoon of unsalted butter over medium heat. Add the chicken and cook, stirring occasionally, until fully cooked, 6 to 8 minutes. Transfer to a medium bowl.

3. Using the same pan, sauté the bell pepper, onion, and garlic over medium heat until softened, 7 to 9 minutes. Add additional butter if needed. Transfer to a bowl.

4. Melt the remaining 3 tablespoons unsalted butter and brush the top side of each tortilla with it. Wipe the skillet clean with paper towels, then place it over medium heat. In a small bowl, toss the cheeses together.

5. Working with one tortilla at a time, transfer each one, buttered-side down, to the skillet. Working quickly, sprinkle ½ cup of the cheese evenly over one half of the tortilla, then sprinkle with about ¾ cup of the chicken mixture. Fold the top half over and repeat with a second tortilla (you can fit two in the skillet at once). Reduce the heat to medium-low and let cook until golden brown on the bottom, about 5 minutes, then carefully turn over and cook until golden brown on bottom, another couple minutes. Repeat the process with the remaining tortillas, cheese, and filling.

6. Cut each quesadilla into 2 or 3 wedges. Serve warm with lime wedges and guacamole, sour cream, and pico de gallo (if using).

Storage: Keep the quesadillas tightly covered in the refrigerator for up to 4 days. Reheat on a parchment paper–covered baking sheet in a 340°F oven for 5 to 7 minutes. You can also microwave them, but you will lose the crispness, which would be sad.

Bacon-Wrapped Poppers

PREP TIME: 10 MINUTES | COOK TIME: 25 MINUTES | YIELD: 8 SERVINGS (2 POPPERS PER SERVING)

THC: 5MG PER SERVING (2.5MG PER POPPER) | GLUTEN-FREE | NUT-FREE

Jalapeños lose some of their bite when cooked. The seeds seem to be the spiciest, so if you want a mild popper, remove all the seeds. In these poppers, the bacon melts into the cheese, and the whole thing is a decidedly delicious cannabis treat.

Nonstick baking spray

8 jalapeño peppers, 3 to 4 inches long

1 (4-ounce) package cream cheese, softened

½ cup shredded Cheddar cheese

4 teaspoons Canna-Butter (page 43), softened

½ teaspoon onion powder

½ teaspoon salt

½ teaspoon freshly ground black pepper

8 slices thin-sliced bacon

1. Preheat the oven to 340°F. Line a baking sheet with parchment paper and coat lightly with nonstick spray.
2. Cut the jalapeños in half lengthwise and use a spoon to scoop out the seeds and ribs. If you have kitchen gloves, this would be a good time to use them.
3. In a medium bowl, mix the cream cheese, Cheddar cheese, canna-butter, onion powder, salt, and pepper together until well combined. Fill each jalapeño half with the cheese mixture.
4. Cut the slices of bacon in half and wrap each pepper half in a slice of bacon, using toothpicks to secure it.
5. Arrange the peppers on the prepared baking sheet and bake until the bacon is crispy and browned, 20 to 25 minutes. Serve immediately.

Storage: Keep in an airtight container or wrapped well in aluminum foil in the refrigerator for 3 to 5 days. Reheat in a 340°F oven for 5 to 6 minutes or in the microwave for 1 minute at 50 percent power.

Shortcut Empanada Bites

PREP TIME: 30 MINUTES | COOK TIME: 46 MINUTES | YIELD: 4 SERVINGS (3 EMPANADAS PER SERVING)
THC: 5MG PER SERVING (1.67MG PER EMPANADA) | **NUT-FREE**

My friend Inez is from Argentina, and she makes the best empanadas I've ever had. This is her recipe (with the addition of cannabis), made into bite-size pies.

1 store-bought refrigerated rolled pie shell

2 tablespoons canola oil

2 teaspoons Canna-Oil (page 47)

1 small onion, finely chopped

2 garlic cloves, minced

12 ounces ground beef or chicken

¼ cup ground chorizo

2 tablespoons tomato paste

1 tablespoon store-bought sofrito

1 teaspoon ground cumin

¼ cup currants or raisins

¼ cup chopped pitted olives

2 tablespoons red wine vinegar

1 large egg, lightly beaten

1. Unroll the pie shell on a floured work surface. Flatten it a bit with a rolling pin. Using a 2-inch biscuit cutter, start at the outside of the crust and cut 12 circles. Line a baking sheet with parchment paper, and place the circles on it. Refrigerate the dough.

2. In a large skillet, heat the oils over medium heat. Cook the onion and garlic, stirring a few times, until tender and lightly browned, 8 to 10 minutes. Add the ground meats and sauté until cooked through, 9 to 10 minutes. Add the tomato paste, sofrito, cumin, currants, olives, and vinegar and cook, stirring, for 5 to 6 minutes. Remove from the heat and let cool.

3. Preheat the oven to 325°F.

4. Remove the pastry from the refrigerator. Place a tablespoon of the mixture in the center of each circle. Fold the dough over and use the tines of a fork to seal completely. Brush the tops with the egg. Bake until golden brown and crisp, about 20 minutes. Serve warm.

Tip: Look for sofrito in the international section of your grocery store. Goya makes a good version that is widely available.

Storage: Keep the empanadas wrapped tightly or in an airtight container in the refrigerator for up to 3 to 4 days or freeze for a month. To reheat, wrap them in foil and place them in a preheated 325°F oven until warm, 7 to 10 minutes.

Charred Brussels Sprouts with Bacon Jam

PREP TIME: 10 MINUTES | COOK TIME: 30 MINUTES | YIELD: 4 SERVINGS | THC: 5MG PER SERVING

DAIRY-FREE | NUT-FREE | GLUTEN-FREE

For years I thought of Brussels sprouts as an absolutely vile vegetable. I'd see them in steam tables, overcooked for hours until they were mushy and forgettable. Thankfully this veggie has begun to see a resurgence. The once off-putting side dish suddenly has crunch to it and is packed with flavor. Now I consider them my favorite side, and this recipe makes the most of their earthy, complex flavor.

2 tablespoons canola oil

1 pound Brussels sprouts, trimmed and halved through the stem end

Salt

Freshly ground black pepper

2 teaspoons Canna-Oil (page 47)

4 ounces thick-cut bacon, cut into ½-inch pieces

1 medium red onion, chopped

1 garlic clove, chopped

¼ cup packed light brown sugar

2 tablespoons fig jam

2 tablespoons apple cider vinegar

1. In a large skillet, heat the canola oil over medium heat. Place the Brussels sprouts in the pan in a single layer. (If your pan is not big enough, cook the sprouts in two batches.) Season with salt and pepper and cook, turning occasionally, until tender and deeply browned, about 10 minutes. If the sprouts start to burn, turn the heat to medium-low. Remove from the heat.

2. In a medium skillet, heat the canna-oil over medium heat. Add the bacon and cook over medium-low heat until just crisp, 7 to 8 minutes. When the bacon is cooked, add the onion and cook until softened, 7 to 9 minutes, stirring frequently. Stir in the garlic. Add the brown sugar, fig jam, and vinegar and stir over medium-low heat until combined.

3. Return the pan with the Brussels sprouts to medium heat and stir for 2 to 3 minutes to reheat.

4. Plate the sprouts and divide the bacon jam between the four servings.

Storage: Keep the sprouts in an airtight container in the refrigerator for 3 to 4 days.

MANY LAYER
BARS, PAGE 77

CHAPTER 5

Where It All Began: Brownies and Other Bars

Our current interest in cannabis-infused food may have been sparked by the 1954 publication of *The Alice B. Toklas Cook Book*. Although her "Haschich Fudge," similar to a dense brownie, was censored from the first American edition, and the recipe was her friend's, with subsequent printings these "brownies" eventually became synonymous with hippies, cannabis, and edibles and were a famous symbol of cannabis love in the '60s.

Cheesecake Brownies

PREP TIME: 10 MINUTES | COOK TIME: 40 MINUTES | YIELD: 12 SERVINGS (1 BROWNIE PER SERVING)

THC: 5MG PER BROWNIE | NUT-FREE | VEGETARIAN

The concept of brownie and cheesecake in the same pan is nothing short of brilliant. The smoothness of the cheesecake and the fudginess of the brownie are a marriage that's gonna last. I love the taste of vanilla that peeks through these wonderful flavors.

Nonstick baking spray

1 (8-ounce) package cream cheese, softened

1¼ cups granulated sugar, divided

3 large eggs, divided

3 teaspoons vanilla extract, divided

6 tablespoons (¾ stick) unsalted butter, softened

2 tablespoons Canna-Butter (page 43), softened

½ cup unsweetened cocoa powder

¾ cup all-purpose flour

½ cup semisweet chocolate chips

¼ teaspoon salt

1. Preheat the oven to 340°F. Line an 8-inch square baking pan with aluminum foil and coat lightly with nonstick spray.

2. In a large bowl, using an electric mixer on medium speed, beat the cream cheese and ¼ cup of sugar together until smooth and creamy. Add 1 egg and 2 teaspoons of vanilla and beat till just blended. Set aside.

3. In a large microwave-safe bowl, melt the butters. Whisk in the remaining 1 cup sugar and the cocoa. Beat in the remaining 2 eggs and 1 teaspoon vanilla until smooth. Stir in the flour, chocolate chips, and salt.

4. Reserve about ½ cup of the brownie batter and spread the rest in the bottom of the prepared pan. Pour the cheesecake mixture over the batter and spread evenly. Drop the reserved brownie batter by the spoonful over the cheesecake filling. Swirl with a butter knife.

5. Bake until the brownies are set, 35 to 40 minutes. Cool completely before cutting into 12 equal pieces.

Storage: Keep the brownies in an airtight container for 5 to 7 days or freeze for several months.

Buttermilk Rocky Road Brownies

PREP TIME: 20 MINUTES | COOK TIME: 35 MINUTES | YIELD: 12 SERVINGS (1 BROWNIE PER SERVING)
THC: 5MG PER BROWNIE

These brownies may be over-the-top, but yes, they are worth it. Growing up, my favorite ice cream flavor was always rocky road. The texture variations of spongy marshmallows and crunchy nuts are the perfect companions in a dark sea of creamy chocolate. While we are going over-the-top, please, please add a scoop of vanilla on top.

Nonstick baking spray

6 tablespoons (¾ stick) unsalted butter, softened

2 tablespoons Canna-Butter (page 43), softened

1 cup granulated sugar

2 large eggs

1 teaspoon vanilla extract

1⅓ cups all-purpose flour

1¼ teaspoons baking powder

¼ teaspoon kosher salt

½ cup whole buttermilk

2 cups mini marshmallows

1½ cups semisweet chocolate chips

1 cup sliced almonds

1. Preheat the oven to 340°F. Coat a 9-inch square baking pan with nonstick spray.

2. In a large bowl, using an electric mixer on medium speed, beat the butters and sugar together until fluffy, 3 to 4 minutes, stopping to scrape down the sides of the bowl. Add the eggs, one at a time, beating well after each addition. Beat in the vanilla.

3. In a medium bowl, whisk together the flour, baking powder, and salt. On low speed, gradually add the flour mixture to the butter mixture, alternating with the buttermilk, beginning and ending with flour mixture and beating until just combined after each addition. Spoon the batter into the prepared pan. In order, top with a layer of marshmallows, chocolate chips, and almonds.

4. Bake until a wooden toothpick inserted in the center comes out clean, 30 to 35 minutes. Cool in the pan for 10 minutes. Remove from the pan and cool completely on a wire rack before cutting into 12 equal pieces.

Storage: Keep the brownies in an airtight container for 5 to 7 days or freeze for up to several months.

Gluten-Free Brownies

PREP TIME: 20 MINUTES | COOK TIME: 35 MINUTES | YIELD: 12 SERVINGS (1 BROWNIE PER SERVING)

THC: 5MG PER BROWNIE | GLUTEN-FREE | NUT-FREE | VEGETARIAN

More and more people are turning to gluten-free options these days. And thankfully it's also now easier to find high-quality gluten-free flour mixes (Bob's Red Mill and King Arthur Flour make some great blends). Just because you're omitting the gluten doesn't mean you have to lose the rich chocolate chewiness you are going for with brownies.

Nonstick cooking spray

10 tablespoons (1¼ sticks) unsalted butter, melted

2 tablespoons Canna-Butter (page 43)

1 cup granulated sugar

½ cup packed light brown sugar

1 teaspoon vanilla extract

3 large eggs, at room temperature

½ cup unsweetened cocoa powder

½ cup gluten-free flour

1 cup chocolate chips

1. Preheat the oven to 340°F. Coat an 8-inch square baking pan with nonstick cooking spray and line with parchment paper with an overhang on two sides so you can easily lift the bars from the pan.

2. In a large bowl, gently whisk the butters and sugars together. Stir in the vanilla. Add the eggs, one at a time, stirring in between each addition. Sift in the cocoa and flour and stir until just combined. Stir in the chocolate chips. Pour the brownie batter into the prepared pan.

3. Bake until the brownies are set in the middle, 30 to 35 minutes. Transfer the pan to a wire rack to cool completely. These brownies are quite fragile, so if you want to speed up the cooling, transfer them to the refrigerator. Once the brownies are completely cool, cut into 12 equal pieces.

Storage: Keep the brownies well wrapped in aluminum foil in the refrigerator for 5 to 7 days or freeze for up to several months.

Pecan Bars

PREP TIME: 20 MINUTES | COOK TIME: 1 HOUR 15 MINUTES | YIELD: 16 SERVINGS (1 BAR PER SERVING)

THC: 5MG PER BAR | VEGETARIAN

These bars have a chewiness that, when done right, is memorable. Topped with crisp toasted pecans, filled with luscious caramel, and finished with a tender, buttery crust, these bars are so rich that we tend to cut them into small squares.

Nonstick baking spray

2 cups plus 2 tablespoons all-purpose flour, divided

½ cup granulated sugar

2 tablespoons plus 2 teaspoons Canna-Butter (page 43)

3½ teaspoons unsalted butter, cut into pieces

¾ teaspoon plus pinch kosher salt, divided

¾ cup packed dark brown sugar

4 large eggs

2 teaspoons vanilla extract

1 cup light corn syrup

2 cups chopped pecans

Pecan halves, for placing on top of the bars

1. Preheat the oven to 340°F. Coat an 8-inch square baking pan with nonstick spray and line with parchment paper with an overhang on two sides so you can easily lift the bars from the pan. (The filling is sticky and can make it hard to remove without the parchment.)

2. In a food processor, pulse 2 cups of flour, the sugar, butters, and ¾ teaspoon of salt until combined. The mixture will form into clumps. Transfer the dough to the prepared pan. Press it firmly and evenly in the bottom of the pan. Pierce the crust all over with a fork and bake until light to medium golden brown, 30 to 35 minutes.

3. Using the same food processor bowl, combine the brown sugar, the remaining 2 tablespoons flour, pinch salt, eggs, vanilla, and corn syrup. (Add the corn syrup last so it doesn't get stuck on the bottom of the food processor.) Pulse until completely combined. Turn the mixture into a large bowl and add the pecans. Spoon the pecan mixture evenly over the baked crust. Place a few extra pecan halves on the top of the filling as decoration.

4. Return the pan to the oven and bake until the center is just set, 35 to 40 minutes. If the center still jiggles, bake for a few more minutes; if you notice the bars starting to puff in the middle, remove them immediately. Cool completely in the pan on a wire rack before cutting into 16 (2-inch) squares and lifting the bars out.

Storage: Keep the bars in an airtight container at room temperature for to 3 to 5 days or freeze for up to 6 months. They can be very sticky, so wrap them in parchment or wax paper.

Lemon-Lime Bars

PREP TIME: 25 MINUTES | COOK TIME: 50 MINUTES | YIELD: 12 SERVINGS (1 BAR PER SERVING)

THC: 5MG PER BAR | NUT-FREE | VEGETARIAN

These bars get their slightly greenish hue from the canna-butter and lime peel in the filling. They are pretty, tangy, and suited for citrus lovers. These always make me think of summertime.

Nonstick baking spray

1 cup all-purpose flour

6 tablespoons (¾ stick) unsalted butter

2 tablespoons Canna-Butter (page 43)

¼ cup confectioners' sugar

1 cup granulated sugar

2 large eggs

1 tablespoon grated lemon zest

2 teaspoons grated lime zest

1 tablespoon freshly squeezed lemon juice

1 tablespoon freshly squeezed lime juice

½ teaspoon baking powder

¼ teaspoon salt

1. Preheat the oven to 340°F. Coat an 8-inch square baking pan with nonstick spray. Line the pan with parchment paper with an overhang on two sides so you can easily lift the bars from the pan.

2. In a small bowl, combine the flour, butters, and confectioners' sugar. Press firmly and evenly into the bottom of the prepared pan. Bake until lightly golden, about 20 minutes.

3. In a medium bowl, combine the sugar, eggs, lemon and lime zests and juices, baking powder, and salt and beat until fluffy. Pour over the crust.

4. Bake until the filling is set, 25 to 30 minutes. Cool completely before carefully lifting the bars out of the pan using the parchment paper. Cut into 12 equal pieces.

Storage: Keep the bars in an airtight container in the refrigerator for 5 to 7 days.

Many Layer Bars

PREP TIME: 30 MINUTES | COOK TIME: 25 MINUTES | YIELD: 12 SERVINGS (1 BAR PER SERVING)

THC: 5MG PER BAR | VEGAN

These are also known as seven-layer or Hello Dolly bars. They take 30 minutes of hands-on prep and call for just eight ingredients, making them the perfect dessert for taking, well, just about anywhere!

1¼ cups graham cracker crumbs

2 tablespoons Canna-Coconut Oil (page 45), melted

1 tablespoon coconut oil, melted

¾ cup vegan chocolate chips

⅔ cup flaked sweetened coconut

⅓ cup chopped pecans, toasted (see Tip on page 79)

⅓ cup chopped walnuts, toasted (see Tip on page 79)

¾ cup sweetened coconut condensed milk

1. Preheat the oven to 340°F. Line the bottom and sides of an 8-inch square baking pan with parchment paper with an overhang on two sides so you can easily lift the bars from the pan.

2. In a medium bowl, mix together the graham cracker crumbs and coconut oils. Gently pat the mixture evenly into the bottom of the prepared pan. In order, sprinkle the chocolate chips, coconut, pecans, and walnuts evenly over the crust. Drizzle the condensed milk evenly over everything.

3. Bake until lightly browned and bubbly around edges, about 25 minutes. Cool completely in the pan on a wire rack before carefully lifting the bars out of the pan using the parchment paper. Cut into 12 equal pieces.

Tip: The bars can create a sticky mess in the pan, so it's crucial to line the pan with parchment paper. Because the milk needs to seep into the graham cracker crumbs, don't pack the crumbs too tightly in the bottom of the pan.

Storage: Keep the bars tightly covered in the refrigerator for up to 1 week or freeze up to 6 months. Defrost them in the refrigerator.

Almond Jam Bars

PREP TIME: 10 MINUTES | COOK TIME: 30 MINUTES | YIELD: 12 SERVINGS (1 BAR PER SERVING)
THC: 5MG PER BAR | VEGETARIAN

Almond extract is a great flavor paired with cannabis. In a moist and chewy cake swirled with tangy raspberry, the flavors all come together magnificently. Perfect with a cup of tea or coffee, day or night.

Nonstick baking spray

2 large eggs

½ cup granulated sugar

½ cup packed light brown sugar

2 tablespoons Canna-Butter (page 43), melted

⅓ cup unsalted butter, melted

1 teaspoon vanilla extract

¼ teaspoon almond extract

1⅓ cups all-purpose flour

½ teaspoon baking powder

¼ teaspoon salt

¼ cup chopped almonds

½ cup raspberry jam

2 tablespoons orange juice

1. Preheat the oven to 340°F. Coat an 8-inch square baking pan with nonstick spray.

2. In a large bowl, using an electric mixer on medium speed, beat the eggs and sugars together until pale and creamy, about 3 minutes. Add the butters and extracts; mix well.

3. In a small bowl, combine the flour, baking powder, and salt. Gradually add to the creamed mixture, beating just until blended, but don't overbeat. Stir in the almonds. Pour the batter into the prepared baking pan.

4. In another small bowl, combine the jam and orange juice. Drizzle the mixture over the batter and use a knife to swirl it into the batter; don't overmix.

5. Bake until a toothpick inserted in the center comes out clean, 25 to 30 minutes. Cool completely in the pan on a wire rack before cutting into 12 equal pieces.

Storage: Keep the bars in an airtight container in the refrigerator; if well sealed, they will last a couple weeks.

Next-Level Crispy Rice Treats

PREP TIME: 10 MINUTES | COOK TIME: 5 MINUTES | YIELD: 20 SERVINGS (1 BAR PER SERVING)

THC: 5MG PER BAR | NUT-FREE

These treats are not just for kids anymore. Versatile and easy to make, they definitely fall into the "comfort food" category. Add chocolate or butterscotch chips if you want another layer of yum.

Nonstick baking spray

6 tablespoons (¾ stick) unsalted butter

3 tablespoons plus 1 teaspoon Canna-Butter (page 43)

8 cups mini marshmallows

1 teaspoon vanilla extract

1¼ teaspoons ground cinnamon, divided

½ teaspoon kosher salt

6 cups Rice Krispies or other crisped rice cereal

1 cup almond slivers, toasted (see Tip below)

½ cup dried cherries

2 tablespoons granulated sugar

1. Line a 9-inch square baking pan with aluminum foil and coat it lightly with nonstick spray.

2. In a large saucepan over medium-low heat, melt the unsalted butter. Once it's melted, continue to cook until it begins to brown, stirring constantly. Once it has browned to an amber color, add the canna-butter and stir until melted. Add the marshmallows and stir constantly until melted, 4 to 5 minutes. Remove from the heat and stir in the vanilla, 1 teaspoon of cinnamon, and the salt. Immediately stir in the cereal, almonds, and cherries until coated evenly with the marshmallow mixture.

3. Pour the mixture into the prepared pan and press evenly. Combine the sugar and remaining ¼ teaspoon cinnamon and sprinkle over the entire mixture. Cool completely before cutting into 20 equal pieces.

Tip: To toast nuts, put them on a baking sheet in a 350°F oven and bake until they are fragrant and start to brown, 3 to 5 minutes.

Storage: Keep your leftovers in an airtight container at room temperature for 3 days or freeze for up to 6 months.

Pumpkin Swirl Bars

PREP TIME: 40 MINUTES | COOK TIME: 38 MINUTES | YIELD: 12 SERVINGS (1 BAR PER SERVING)

THC: 5MG PER BAR | NUT-FREE | VEGETARIAN

These pumpkin bars are light and spicy and perfect for fall, without the usual heaviness of holiday treats. Maple syrup sweetens this treat while adding great flavor. The bars are topped with crumble and glazed to perfection.

FOR THE BARS

Nonstick baking spray

¼ cup packed light brown sugar

¼ cup maple syrup

2 tablespoons Canna-Butter (page 43), melted and cooled to room temperature

2 tablespoons unsalted butter, melted and cooled to room temperature

2 tablespoons vanilla Greek yogurt

1 (15-ounce) can pumpkin purée

3 large eggs, at room temperature and lightly beaten

1 teaspoon vanilla extract

2 teaspoons baking powder

1½ teaspoons pumpkin pie spice

1. Preheat the oven to 340°F. Coat a 9-inch square baking pan with nonstick spray.

2. For the cake, in a large bowl, whisk the brown sugar, maple syrup, butters, and yogurt together to combine. Stir in the pumpkin, eggs, and vanilla until smooth and well combined. Sprinkle the baking powder, pumpkin pie spice, cinnamon, and salt over the top. Then, sprinkle on the two flours. Stir just until the flour disappears. Scrape into the prepared baking dish and smooth the top.

3. For the crumble, in a small bowl, combine the flour, brown sugar, and cinnamon. Pour the butter over the top. With a fork or your fingers, stir together until crumbs form. Sprinkle over the top of the batter.

4. Bake until the center is set and springs back lightly when touched and a toothpick inserted in the center comes out clean, 35 to 38 minutes. Let cool completely in the pan on a wire rack.

1 teaspoon ground cinnamon

½ teaspoon kosher salt

1½ cups white whole wheat flour

1 cup all-purpose flour

FOR THE CRUMBLE

½ cup all-purpose flour

3 tablespoons packed light brown sugar

½ teaspoon ground cinnamon

3 tablespoons unsalted butter, melted

FOR THE GLAZE

1 tablespoon unsalted butter

¾ cup confectioners' sugar

1 tablespoon maple syrup

1 teaspoon milk (any kind you like; I use unsweetened almond milk), plus more as needed

5. For the glaze, in a microwave-safe bowl or small saucepan, melt the butter. Stir in the confectioners' sugar. Once it is as combined as it can be (it will still be dry and clumpy), whisk in the maple syrup. If you have any trouble combining them, microwave the bowl in short 15-second bursts (or heat on the stove over medium-low) until you have a smooth frosting. Stir in the milk and try not to eat the whole bowl with a spoon. If you'd like a glaze with thinner consistency, add additional milk, 1 teaspoon at a time, until your desired consistency is reached.

6. Drizzle over the bars. Once completely cool, slice into 12 even bars and dive on in!

Storage: Keep the bars in an airtight container in the refrigerator for 5 to 7 days or freeze for up to several months.

Toffee Shortbread Bars

PREP TIME: 40 MINUTES | COOK TIME: 35 MINUTES | YIELD: 16 SERVINGS (1 BAR PER SERVING)
THC: 5MG PER BAR | VEGETARIAN

Rich, buttery shortbread with chocolate toffee bits makes for a satisfying treat in small doses. It is simple but decadent.

Nonstick baking spray

1½ cups all-purpose flour

½ teaspoon baking powder

1 teaspoon salt, divided

10 tablespoons (1¼ sticks) unsalted butter, softened

2 tablespoons plus 2 teaspoons Canna-Butter (page 43), softened

¾ cup packed light brown sugar

1 large egg, at room temperature

1 teaspoon vanilla extract

6 ounces chocolate toffee bar, chopped

1. Preheat the oven to 325°F. Line an 8-inch square baking pan with an overhang on two sides so you can easily lift the bars from the pan; lightly coat with nonstick spray.

2. In a medium bowl, whisk together the flour, baking powder, and ½ teaspoon of salt; set aside.

3. In a large bowl, using an electric mixer on medium-high speed, beat the butters and sugar together until light and fluffy, 3 to 4 minutes. Beat in the egg and vanilla until combined. Reduce the speed to low and gradually add the flour mixture, mixing until just combined.

4. Spread the batter in the prepared pan and bake until a toothpick inserted in the center comes out clean, 30 to 35 minutes.

5. Remove the pan from the oven and scatter the toffee pieces evenly over the top. Return to the oven and bake until the toffee is melted, 1 to 2 minutes more. Sprinkle with the remaining ½ teaspoon salt.

6. Cool completely in the pan. Holding the paper overhang, lift the bars out of the pan and transfer to a cutting board. Cut into 16 equal squares.

Storage: Keep the bars in an airtight container at room temperature for 5 to 7 days or freeze for up to several months.

CHERRY AND WHITE
CHOCOLATE CHUNK
COOKIES, PAGE 90

CHAPTER 6

Canna-Cookies

I've never met a person who doesn't like a cookie. There are so many varieties: chewy, crunchy, and filled with all sorts of goodies. Keep your eye on the cookies while they are in the oven, as a couple of minutes can make the difference between a good cookie and a great one. If you like your cookies soft, take them out at the low end of the suggested times. Also, check your oven temperature before baking. You can buy inexpensive oven thermometers to take out the guesswork. Most cookies freeze well for extended freshness. I like to take one or two out of the freezer and let them come to room temperature for a late-night infusion. Also, note that while most cookies listed here use wheat flour, many of them can be made gluten-free simply by swapping in your preferred brand of all-purpose gluten-free flour.

Oatmeal-Date Cookies

PREP TIME: 15 MINUTES | COOK TIME: 12 MINUTES | YIELD: 24 COOKIES (2 COOKIES PER SERVING)

THC: 5MG PER SERVING (2.5MG PER COOKIE) | NUT-FREE | VEGETARIAN

Dates add a sweetness to baked goods that is divine, and the hint of cardamom in this recipe adds a lovely layer of complexity. I love these cookies with a cup of spiced tea, like chai.

1¾ cups old-fashioned rolled oats

1 cup chopped dates

¾ cup all-purpose flour

¾ teaspoon ground cinnamon

½ teaspoon baking soda

½ teaspoon salt

½ teaspoon ground cardamom

10 tablespoons (1¼ sticks) unsalted butter, softened

2 tablespoons Canna-Butter (page 43), softened

⅓ cup packed light brown sugar

⅓ cup granulated sugar

1 large egg, at room temperature

½ teaspoon vanilla extract

1. Preheat the oven to 340°F. Adjust the racks to the upper and lower thirds of the oven. Line two baking sheets with parchment paper.

2. In a medium bowl, stir together the oats, dates, flour, cinnamon, baking soda, salt, and cardamom.

3. In a large bowl, using an electric mixer on medium speed, beat together the butters, brown sugar, and granulated sugar until light and fluffy. Add the egg and vanilla and beat until well combined. Add the oat mixture and beat until just combined.

4. Drop the dough by heaping tablespoons, 2 inches apart, onto the prepared baking sheets and flatten the mounds slightly with moistened fingers.

5. Bake, switching the position of the sheets halfway through baking, until golden, about 12 minutes. Transfer the cookies to wire racks to cool.

Storage: Keep the cookies in an airtight container for up to 1 week or freeze for up to 6 months.

Creamsicle Cookies

PREP TIME: 10 MINUTES | COOK TIME: 10 MINUTES | YIELD: 24 COOKIES (2 LARGE COOKIES PER SERVING) | THC: 5MG PER SERVING (2.5MG PER COOKIE) | NUT-FREE | VEGETARIAN

These cookies remind me of an Orange Julius, a frosty blended drink from my childhood, a thousand years ago. Orange and vanilla are a winning combo. These cookies are light, fruity, and easy to make.

14 tablespoons (1¾ sticks) unsalted butter, softened

2 tablespoons Canna-Butter (page 43), softened

½ cup granulated sugar

½ cup packed light brown sugar

1 large egg, at room temperature

1½ tablespoons orange juice

2¼ cups all-purpose flour

2 tablespoons grated orange zest

1 teaspoon baking soda

½ teaspoon salt

2 cups white chocolate chips

1. Preheat the oven to 340°F. Line two baking sheets with parchment paper.

2. In a large bowl, using an electric mixer on medium speed, beat the butters and both sugars together for about 2 minutes. Add the egg and orange juice and mix for 30 seconds. Add the flour, zest, baking soda, and salt, and mix on low speed, increasing to medium-low speed, until the dough comes together. Stir in the chocolate chips until incorporated. Drop heaping 2-tablespoon scoops of the dough 2 inches apart onto the prepared baking sheets.

3. Bake until the edges are lightly golden, 8 to 10 minutes. Let cool for 3 minutes on the baking sheet, then transfer the cookies to a wire rack to finish cooling.

Storage: Keep the cookies in an airtight container for 4 to 5 days or freeze for up to 6 months.

Chunky Peanut Butter Cookies

**PREP TIME: 20 MINUTES | COOK TIME: 12 MINUTES | YIELD: 24 COOKIES
(2 COOKIES PER SERVING) | THC: 5MG PER SERVING (2.5MG PER COOKIE) | VEGETARIAN**

These soft peanut butter cookies are easy to make, full of peanut butter flavor, and don't require any dough chilling! Sandwich some ice cream between a couple and you won't be sorry.

1½ cups all-purpose flour

½ teaspoon baking soda

¼ teaspoon salt

6 tablespoons (¾ stick) unsalted butter, softened

2 tablespoons Canna-Butter (page 43), softened

¾ cup packed light brown sugar

¼ cup plus 3 tablespoons granulated sugar, divided

¾ cup chunky peanut butter

1 large egg, at room temperature

1 teaspoon vanilla extract

1. Preheat the oven to 340°F. Line two baking sheets with parchment paper.

2. In a medium bowl, whisk together the flour, baking soda, and salt. Set aside.

3. In a large bowl, using an electric mixer on medium speed, beat the butters, brown sugar, and ¼ cup of granulated sugar together until well combined, 1 to 2 minutes. Add the peanut butter and mix until well combined, stopping to scrape down the sides of the bowl as needed. Beat in the egg and vanilla until fully combined. On low speed, add the dry ingredients and mix until just combined.

4. Place the remaining 3 tablespoons of granulated sugar in a small bowl. Using a 2-tablespoon cookie scoop, scoop the dough from the bowl, roll each scoop into a ball, and coat in the granulated sugar. Place each ball of cookie dough on the prepared baking sheets, spacing them about 2 inches apart. Gently press down with a fork on the top of each cookie to make a small crisscross pattern.

5. Bake until the tops are set, 10 to 12 minutes. Remove from the oven and cool on the baking sheet for 5 to 10 minutes, then carefully transfer the cookies to a wire rack to finish cooling.

Storage: Keep the cookies in an airtight container for 4 to 5 days or freeze for up to 6 months.

Brown Butter Dreams

PREP TIME: 10 MINUTES PLUS 30 MINUTES CHILL TIME | COOK TIME: 19 MINUTES | YIELD: 24 COOKIES (2 COOKIES PER SERVING) | THC: 5MG PER COOKIES (2.5MG PER COOKIE) | NUT-FREE | VEGETARIAN

If you have never tasted a cookie baked with brown butter you are in for a treat. It's nutty and caramelly and hard to resist.

6 tablespoons (¾ stick) unsalted butter

2 tablespoons Canna-Butter (page 43)

1 cup packed light brown sugar

1 large egg, at room temperature

1 tablespoon spiced rum

1¼ cups all-purpose flour

1½ teaspoons ground cinnamon

½ teaspoon baking soda

¼ teaspoon salt

¼ teaspoon ground ginger

¼ teaspoon ground nutmeg

½ cup semisweet chocolate mini chips

Nonstick baking spray

1. In a small heavy saucepan, cook the unsalted butter over medium heat until golden brown, 5 to 7 minutes; cool slightly, then stir in the canna-butter until melted.
2. In a large bowl, beat the brown sugar and browned butter together until blended. Beat in the egg, then the rum.
3. In a medium bowl, combine the flour, cinnamon, baking soda, salt, ginger, and nutmeg. Gradually add to the brown sugar mixture and mix well. Stir in the chocolate chips. Cover and refrigerate for at least 30 minutes and up to 2 days.
4. Preheat the oven to 340°F. Coat two baking sheets with nonstick spray.
5. Drop rounded tablespoons of the dough 2 inches apart onto the prepared baking sheets. Bake until the bottoms are lightly browned, 10 to 12 minutes. Transfer the cookies to wire racks to cool.

Storage: Keep the cookies in an airtight container for 4 to 5 days or freeze for up to 6 months.

Cherry and White Chocolate Chunk Cookies

PREP TIME: 10 MINUTES | COOK TIME: 12 MINUTES | YIELD: 18 COOKIES (2 COOKIES PER SERVING)

THC: 5MG PER SERVING (2.5MG PER COOKIE) | NUT-FREE | VEGETARIAN

Cherry, white chocolate, and cannabis is a winning threesome. I love when they are warm. I like to heat them in the microwave for 10 seconds, just long enough for the chocolate to melt. These are so comforting and totally satisfying.

6½ tablespoons unsalted butter, softened

1½ tablespoons Canna-Butter (page 43), softened

⅔ cup granulated sugar

1 large egg

1 teaspoon vanilla extract

1 cup plus 2 tablespoons all-purpose flour

½ teaspoon baking soda

1 cup dried cherries

1 cup white chocolate chunks

1. Preheat the oven to 340°F.
2. In a large bowl, using an electric mixer on medium speed, cream the butters and sugar together until light and fluffy. Beat in the egg and vanilla.
3. In a small bowl, whisk the flour and baking soda together; gradually beat into the creamed mixture. Stir in the cherries and chocolate chunks. Drop the dough by heaping teaspoons 2 inches apart onto ungreased baking sheets.
4. Bake until golden brown, 10 to 12 minutes. Cool on the baking sheets for 1 minute, then transfer the cookies to wire racks to cool completely.

Storage: Keep the cookies in an airtight container for 4 to 5 days or freeze for up to 6 months.

Sugar Cookies

PREP TIME: 20 MINUTES PLUS 2 HOURS CHILL TIME | COOK TIME: 16 MINUTES | YIELD: 30 COOKIES (2 COOKIES PER SERVING) | THC: 5MG PER SERVING (2.5MG PER COOKIE) | NUT-FREE | VEGETARIAN

It should be a law that everyone has to have a cannabis-infused rollable sugar cookie recipe. What would the holidays be without it! Check out all the fun cookie decorations available these days—the possibilities are endless.

3 cups all-purpose flour, plus more for rolling

¾ teaspoon kosher salt

½ teaspoon baking powder

1 cup (2 sticks) plus 1½ tablespoons unsalted butter, chilled and cubed

2½ tablespoons Canna-Butter (page 43), chilled and cubed

1 cup granulated sugar

1 large egg

1 large egg yolk

1 teaspoon vanilla extract

1. In a small bowl, whisk the flour, salt, and baking powder.
2. In a large bowl, using an electric mixer on high speed, beat the butters and sugar together until well combined (the butter does not need to be fluffy), about 3 minutes. Add the egg, egg yolk, and vanilla; beat just to combine. Reduce the mixer speed to low and gradually add the dry ingredients; mix just to combine.
3. Form the dough into 2 (¾-inch-thick) disks and wrap in plastic. Chill for at least 2 hours.
4. Preheat the oven to 325°F. Adjust the racks to the lower and upper thirds of the oven. Line two baking sheets with parchment paper.
5. Let 1 disk of dough sit at room temperature until softened slightly, about 5 minutes. Roll out on a lightly floured sheet of parchment until it's about ¼-inch thick, dusting with flour as needed (if the dough gets soft or sticky, chill on the parchment until firm). Cut out shapes with floured cookie cutters; transfer to the prepared sheets.
6. Bake, rotating the baking sheets top to bottom and back to front halfway through, until the edges are golden, 12 to 16 minutes. Transfer the cookies to wire racks to cool. Repeat Steps 5 and 6 with the scraps and remaining dough.

Storage: Keep the cookies in an airtight container for 2 weeks or freeze for up to 6 months.

Spicy Molasses Cookies

PREP TIME: 30 MINUTES PLUS 1 HOUR CHILL TIME | COOK TIME: 12 MINUTES | YIELD: 20 COOKIES (2 COOKIES PER SERVING) | THC: 5MG PER SERVING (2.5MG PER COOKIE) | NUT-FREE | VEGETARIAN

We love a spicy cookie. This perfumed recipe is perfect with a cup of tea and a good book. Relax, eat your cookies, and let the fun begin.

1¼ cups all-purpose flour

½ cup whole wheat flour

2 teaspoons ground ginger

2 teaspoons ground cinnamon

1½ teaspoons finely ground black pepper, plus more for sprinkling

1 teaspoon baking soda

1 teaspoon kosher salt

¾ teaspoon ground cloves

1 cup packed dark brown sugar

6 tablespoons plus 1 teaspoon unsalted butter, softened

5 teaspoons Canna-Butter (page 43), softened

1 large egg, at room temperature

⅓ cup plus 1 tablespoon light molasses, divided

¾ cup confectioners' sugar

1 tablespoon milk

Raw sugar, for sprinkling

1. In a medium bowl, whisk the flours, ginger, cinnamon, pepper, baking soda, salt, and cloves together. Set aside.

2. In a large bowl, using an electric mixer on medium speed, beat the brown sugar and butters together until light and fluffy, about 3 minutes. Add the egg and beat to incorporate. Add ⅓ cup of molasses and mix just to combine. Reduce the mixer speed to low and gradually add the dry ingredients; beat until just incorporated.

3. Pat the dough together and wrap in plastic. Chill until firm, about 1 hour.

4. Preheat the oven to 340°F. Adjust the racks to the upper and lower thirds of the oven. Line two baking sheets with parchment paper.

5. Scoop out level tablespoons of dough and roll between the palms of your hands to make smooth balls. Place on the prepared baking sheets about 2 inches apart.

6. Bake the cookies, rotating the baking sheets top to bottom and back to front halfway through, until just firm around the edges, 9 to 12 minutes (if you like chewier cookies, bake less, and if a crispier cookie is your thing, bake a little longer). Let the cookies cool about 5 minutes on the baking sheets, then transfer to wire racks and cool completely. Repeat with the remaining dough, using fresh parchment paper on the baking sheets.

7. In a medium bowl, whisk the confectioners' sugar, milk, and the remaining 1 tablespoon of molasses together until smooth. The glaze should be very thick and glossy but still pourable. If needed, add more milk or water ½ teaspoon at a time until you get to the right consistency. Drizzle the glaze over the cookies and sprinkle with raw sugar and more pepper.

Storage: Keep the cookies in an airtight container for 4 to 5 days or freeze (unglazed) for up to 6 months.

Double Chocolate Vegan Cookies

PREP TIME: 20 MINUTES | COOK TIME: 10 MINUTES | YIELD: 24 COOKIES (2 COOKIES PER SERVING)
THC: 5MG PER SERVING (2.5MG PER COOKIE) | VEGAN

Both quick and easy, crunchy and soft, these vegan cookies are perfect for satisfying all your chocolate cravings. Vegan options have come a long, long way. Isn't that nice?

6 tablespoons vegan butter

2 tablespoons Canna-Coconut Oil (page 45)

½ cup granulated sugar

½ cup packed light brown sugar

2 teaspoons vanilla extract

1 cup all-purpose flour

⅔ cup unsweetened cocoa powder

1 teaspoon baking soda

¼ teaspoon salt

1 tablespoon almond milk or other nondairy milk

3½ ounces vegan chocolate, plus more for topping, chopped into small chunks

1. Preheat the oven to 340°F. Line two baking sheets with parchment paper.

2. In a large bowl, using an electric mixer on medium speed, cream the vegan butter, canna-coconut oil, and both sugars together. Beat in the vanilla.

3. In a medium bowl, sift the flour and cocoa together, then mix in the baking soda and salt. Stir the dry ingredients into the wet, mixing by hand, until crumbly. Add the almond milk and continue to mix by hand until a thick cookie dough forms. Stir in the chocolate chunks. The dough will be very thick, but sticky enough to easily roll into balls. Roll the dough into tablespoon-size balls and place 2 inches apart on the prepared baking sheets.

4. Bake until the edges are firm, about 10 minutes. The cookies will still be soft in the middle. This is fine; they will firm up as they cool. Press in a few more chocolate chunks to the top of the cookies as they come out of the oven if you like.

5. Allow the cookies to cool for at least 15 minutes on the baking sheet on a wire rack. Cool completely before storing.

Storage: Keep the cookies in an airtight container for 4 to 5 days or freeze for up to 6 months.

Magical Almond Cookies

PREP TIME: 10 MINUTES | COOK TIME: 10 MINUTES | YIELD: 20 COOKIES (2 COOKIES PER SERVING)
THC: 5MG PER SERVING (2.5MG PER COOKIE) | GLUTEN-FREE | VEGAN

Chewy and sweet, these almond cookies are difficult to resist. The almond flavor paired with maple syrup is so yummy, and the texture of this cookie rocks.

2 cups almond meal

⅛ teaspoon baking soda

⅛ teaspoon salt

⅓ cup maple syrup

5 teaspoons Canna-Coconut Oil (page 45), melted

1 teaspoon vanilla extract

½ teaspoon almond extract

1. Preheat the oven to 340°F. Line two baking sheets with parchment paper.

2. In a large bowl, combine the almond meal, baking soda, and salt.

3. In small bowl, combine the maple syrup, canna-coconut oil, vanilla, and almond extract. Add the wet ingredients to the dry and stir to combine. The dough will be sticky and hard to stir. If necessary, add a couple teaspoons of water so it holds together.

4. Roll the dough into 20 (1-inch) balls. Using your hands, press the balls down into flat disks. Place the cookies on the prepared baking sheets 2 inches apart.

5. Bake until golden brown, about 8 minutes. Let the cookies cool completely on the baking sheets.

Storage: Keep the cookies in an airtight container for 4 to 5 days or freeze for up to 6 months.

Breakfast Cookies

PREP TIME: 10 MINUTES | COOK TIME: 16 MINUTES | YIELD: 12 COOKIES (2 COOKIES PER SERVING)
THC: 5MG PER SERVING (2.5MG PER COOKIE) | GLUTEN-FREE | VEGAN

You heard that right—breakfast cookies. Loaded with bananas, oats, and peanut butter, these cookies are a great way to start the day. Or end it. Or both! There are no refined sugars or flours, just nuts, fruits, spices, and oats. And cannabis. You can store them in the freezer for a quick on-the-go breakfast or snack anytime.

2 medium bananas, mashed

1 cup peanut butter or other nut butter

¼ cup maple syrup

1 teaspoon Canna-Coconut Oil (page 45)

1 teaspoon vanilla extract

1 teaspoon ground cinnamon

¼ teaspoon salt

2½ cups old-fashioned rolled oats

½ cup golden raisins

½ cup chopped almonds

1. Preheat the oven to 325°F. Line a baking sheet with parchment paper.

2. In a large bowl, using an electric mixer on medium speed, beat together the bananas, peanut butter, maple syrup, canna-coconut oil, vanilla, cinnamon, and salt until well combined. Add the oats, raisins, and almonds and mix to combine. Scoop ¼-cup portions of the dough onto the prepared baking sheet, flattening each cookie slightly.

3. Bake until golden brown but still soft, 14 to 16 minutes. Let cool on the baking sheet for 5 minutes, then transfer to a wire rack to cool completely.

Storage: Keep the cookies in an airtight container for 4 to 5 days or freeze for up to 6 months.

STRAWBERRY SWIRL
CAKE, PAGE 106

CHAPTER 7

You Baked Me a Cake!

Nothing quite says love like a freshly baked-from-scratch cake. They are great for sharing, gifting, or enjoying all by yourself. Most of the cakes in this section are baked in 8-inch or 9-inch square pans. They're not too big and most will freeze well, so don't feel like you must eat the whole thing. Using parchment paper or nonstick baking spray should prevent any difficulty removing the cakes from the pans. Anyone who has spent some time baking has probably had to deal with not being able to get the whole cake out of the pan. If that happens, keep the crumbs and sprinkle over the cake, or on the ice cream topping the cake, for an extra taste and texture sensation.

Mocha Cupcakes

PREP TIME: 15 MINUTES | COOK TIME: 18 MINUTES | YIELD: 12 SERVINGS (1 CUPCAKE PER SERVING)

THC: 5MG PER CUPCAKE | NUT-FREE | VEGETARIAN

This recipe makes a dozen deeply rich and satisfying cupcakes. Coffee and chocolate are always a beautiful flavor combo, with the richness of the chocolate enhanced by the coffee. These cupcakes will surely win praise and may even help you make some new friends.

FOR THE CUPCAKES

6 tablespoons (¾ stick) unsalted butter

2 tablespoons Canna-Butter (page 43)

2 ounces semisweet chocolate

1 heaping tablespoon instant coffee

¾ cup all-purpose flour

½ cup unsweetened cocoa powder

¾ teaspoon baking powder

½ teaspoon baking soda

¼ teaspoon salt

2 large eggs, at room temperature

½ cup packed light brown sugar

¼ cup granulated sugar

2 teaspoons vanilla extract

½ cup buttermilk

1. Preheat the oven to 340°F. Line a standard 12-count muffin pan with cupcake liners.

2. In a large microwave-safe bowl, melt the butters and chocolate in the microwave. Heat in 30-second increments, stirring between each time. Stir until combined, then mix in the instant coffee. Set aside to cool.

3. In a medium bowl, whisk the flour, cocoa, baking powder, baking soda, and salt together until thoroughly combined. Set aside.

4. In a large bowl, whisk the eggs, both sugars, and vanilla together until smooth. Add the cooled chocolate mixture and whisk until smooth. Mix in half of the flour mixture, then half of the buttermilk. Repeat until everything is added. Stir until just combined; do not overmix. The batter will have a pudding-like consistency.

5. Divide the batter between the cups of the cupcake pan. Bake until a toothpick inserted in the center comes out clean, 16 to 18 minutes. Allow to cool completely before frosting.

FOR THE FROSTING

1 cup (2 sticks) unsalted butter, softened

3 to 4 cups confectioners' sugar

¼ cup heavy cream

1 tablespoon strong brewed coffee, chilled

1 teaspoon vanilla extract

¼ teaspoon salt

6. For the frosting, in a large bowl, using an electric mixer on medium speed, beat the butter until smooth and creamy, about 3 minutes. Reduce the mixer speed to low and beat in the confectioners' sugar, cream, coffee, vanilla, and salt. Increase the mixer speed to high and beat for 3 minutes. Frost the cupcakes once completely cooled.

Storage: Keep the cupcakes covered tightly at room temperature and frost the day you plan to serve them. You can freeze unfrosted cupcakes for up to 3 months. The frosting can be frozen separately as well. Let it thaw in the refrigerator before topping your cupcakes.

Vegan Oatmeal Cake

PREP TIME: 10 MINUTES | COOK TIME: 20 MINUTES | YIELD: 12 SERVINGS (1 PIECE PER SERVING)

THC: 5MG PER SERVING | NUT-FREE | VEGAN

This cake is the ultimate brunch item. It's satisfying and rich without being too sweet. I like baking it the day before. I think it tastes better. That way you can eat it the minute you roll out of bed.

FOR THE CAKE

Nonstick baking spray

1½ cups all-purpose flour

1 cup quick-cooking oats

2 tablespoons packed light brown sugar

2 teaspoons baking powder

½ teaspoon baking soda

1½ cups coconut milk

2 teaspoons vanilla extract

½ teaspoon salt

FOR THE FILLING/TOPPING

⅓ cup all-purpose flour

⅓ cup packed light brown sugar

¼ cup quick-cooking oats

1 teaspoon ground cinnamon

2 tablespoons coconut oil, chilled

2 tablespoons Canna-Coconut Oil (page 45), chilled

1. Preheat the oven to 340°F. Coat an 8-inch square baking pan with nonstick spray.

2. For the cake, in a medium bowl, combine the flour, oats, brown sugar, baking powder, and baking soda.

3. In a large bowl, combine the coconut milk, vanilla, and salt. Add the dry ingredients to the wet ingredients and mix just until combined. Set aside.

4. For the filling/topping, in a small bowl, combine the flour, brown sugar, oats, and cinnamon. Cut in the chilled oils until crumbly and well combined.

5. Spread half of the cake batter over the bottom of the prepared pan. Sprinkle half of the filling/topping over the batter. Gently spread the rest of the cake batter on top of the filling/topping.

6. Bake for 10 minutes. Sprinkle over the remaining filling/topping and bake until it begins to toast, another 10 minutes. Cool completely in the pan on a wire rack before removing and cutting into 12 equal pieces.

Storage: This cake stays moist wrapped in an airtight container for up to a week. It also freezes beautifully for up to 6 months.

Banana-Coconut Bread

PREP TIME: 10 MINUTES | COOK TIME: 50 MINUTES | YIELD: 12 SERVINGS (1 PIECE PER SERVING)

THC: 5MG PER SERVING | NUT-FREE | VEGETARIAN

My favorite banana bread recipe gets baked in a square pan and sprinkled with sugar to create a crunchy topping. The toasted coconut adds even more texture to this moist, flavorful treat.

Nonstick baking spray (optional)

6 tablespoons (¾ stick) unsalted butter, melted and cooled

2 tablespoons Canna-Butter (page 43), melted and cooled

1 cup packed light brown sugar

2 large eggs, at room temperature, lightly beaten

2 teaspoons vanilla extract

1½ cups mashed very ripe bananas (4 to 5)

1¾ cups all-purpose flour

1 teaspoon baking soda

½ teaspoon salt

½ cup shredded sweetened coconut, toasted (see Tip)

¼ cup granulated sugar

1. Preheat the oven to 340°F. Coat an 8-inch square baking pan with nonstick spray or line with parchment paper with an overhang on two sides.

2. In a large bowl, using an electric mixer on medium speed, beat the butters, brown sugar, eggs, and vanilla together until well blended. Mix in the bananas until combined.

3. In a medium bowl, whisk together the flour, baking soda, and salt. Add the dry ingredients to the wet ingredients and stir until just combined. Stir in the coconut. Pour the batter into the prepared pan. Sprinkle the granulated sugar evenly over the top.

4. Bake until a toothpick inserted into the center comes out clean, 45 to 50 minutes. Let the bread cool for about 30 minutes in the pan on a wire rack. Remove from the pan and cut into 12 equal pieces to serve.

Tip: To toast shredded coconut, spread it on a baking sheet and bake at 325°F until golden brown, 5 to 10 minutes.

Storage: The bread will stay moist wrapped or in an airtight container for up to a week. This recipe freezes beautifully for up to 6 months.

Blueberry Buckle

PREP TIME: 10 MINUTES | COOK TIME: 50 MINUTES | YIELD: 12 SERVINGS (1 PIECE PER SERVING)

THC: 5MG PER SERVING | NUT-FREE | VEGETARIAN

Try to use fresh blueberries when they are in season, though frozen will work, too. This cake is homey and satisfying.

FOR THE BUCKLE

Nonstick baking spray

2 tablespoons unsalted butter, softened

2 tablespoons Canna-Butter (page 43), softened

¾ cup granulated sugar

1 large egg, at room temperature

2 cups all-purpose flour

2 teaspoons baking powder

¼ teaspoon salt

½ cup milk

2 cups fresh blueberries

FOR THE TOPPING

⅔ cup granulated sugar

½ cup all-purpose flour

½ teaspoon ground cinnamon

⅓ cup cold unsalted butter, cubed

1. Preheat the oven to 340°F. Coat a 9-inch square baking pan with nonstick spray.

2. For the buckle, in a large bowl, using an electric mixer on medium speed, cream the butters and sugar together until light and fluffy. Beat in the egg.

3. In a medium bowl, combine the flour, baking powder, and salt; add to the creamed mixture alternately with the milk, beating well after each addition. Fold in the blueberries. Pour the batter into the prepared pan.

4. For the topping, in a small bowl, combine the sugar, flour, and cinnamon. Cut in the butter until crumbly. Sprinkle evenly over the batter. Bake until a toothpick inserted in the center comes out clean, 45 to 50 minutes. Cool completely in the pan on a wire rack. Cut into 12 equal pieces and serve from the pan.

Storage: The cake will stay moist wrapped in the refrigerator for 7 days. It freezes beautifully for up to 6 months.

Lemon Poppyseed Loaf

PREP TIME: 10 MINUTES | COOK TIME: 1 HOUR | YIELD: 9 SERVINGS (1 SLICE PER SERVING)

THC: 5MG PER SLICE | NUT-FREE | VEGETARIAN

The refreshing taste of lemon and the occasional crunch of poppy seeds makes this perfect for a cannabis-infused teatime, although there is nothing to prevent you from starting the day with a slice of this tart treat. I also have made the cake with orange zest and juice in place of the lemon. Also delicious.

Nonstick baking spray

Grated zest of 2 lemons

1 cup granulated sugar

½ cup buttermilk or sour cream

¼ cup plus 4 teaspoons freshly squeezed lemon juice, divided

3 large eggs, at room temperature

1¾ cups all-purpose flour

1½ teaspoons baking powder

¼ teaspoon baking soda

¼ teaspoon fine sea salt

7 tablespoons plus 1 teaspoon canola oil

1½ tablespoons Canna-Oil (page 47), melted

2 tablespoons poppy seeds

½ cup confectioners' sugar

1. Preheat the oven to 340°F. Coat an 8-inch loaf pan with nonstick spray.

2. In a large bowl, combine the zest with the sugar, rubbing the mixture between your fingers until it looks like wet sand. Whisk in the buttermilk, ¼ cup of lemon juice, and the eggs.

3. In a medium bowl, whisk together the flour, baking powder, baking soda, and salt. Whisk the dry ingredients into the sugar mixture, then whisk in the oils and poppy seeds. Pour the batter into the prepared pan.

4. Bake until a toothpick inserted in the center comes out clean, about 1 hour. Let cool in the pan until warm to the touch, then turn it out onto a wire rack set over a rimmed baking sheet. Turn the cake right-side up.

5. In a small bowl, whisk together the remaining 4 teaspoons lemon juice and the confectioners' sugar. Use a pastry brush to spread the glaze evenly over the top and sides of cake. Cool completely before cutting into 9 equal slices.

Storage: Keep the loaf tightly wrapped in the refrigerator 5 to 7 days. Due to the glaze, freezing this is challenging (it gets sticky).

Strawberry Swirl Cake

PREP TIME: 15 MINUTES | COOK TIME: 40 MINUTES | YIELD: 12 SERVINGS (1 PIECE PER SERVING)
THC: 5MG PER SERVING | GLUTEN-FREE | VEGETARIAN

This cake has a fabulous moist texture and the flavor pairing of almond and strawberry is phenomenal. And it's gluten-free. How about that? Look for gluten-free 1-to-1 baking flour at natural food stores, online, or a well-stocked supermarket. The formulation will ensure that this cake bakes wonderfully and is an equal substitution for all-purpose flour in recipes.

Nonstick baking spray

10 tablespoons (1¼ sticks) unsalted butter, melted

2 tablespoons Canna-Butter (page 43), melted

1¼ cups plus 2 tablespoons granulated sugar, divided

2 large eggs, lightly beaten

1 tablespoon orange juice concentrate

2 teaspoons grated orange zest

½ teaspoon almond extract

1½ cups gluten-free 1-to-1 baking flour

½ cup plus 1 tablespoon strawberry jam, divided

1 cup slivered or sliced almonds

1½ cups vanilla Greek yogurt

1. Preheat the oven to 340°F. Coat a 9-inch square baking pan with nonstick spray.
2. In a large bowl, combine the melted butters and 1¼ cups of sugar. Stir in the beaten eggs and mix well. Stir in the orange juice concentrate, zest, and almond extract. Stir in the flour until just mixed. Pour the batter into the prepared pan. Using a knife, swirl ½ cup of the jam into the batter toward the center. Sprinkle with the almonds, then the remaining 2 tablespoons sugar.
3. Bake until golden and set, 35 to 40 minutes. Once completely cooled, slice into 12 equal pieces.
4. In a small bowl, combine the yogurt with the remaining 1 tablespoon jam and place a dollop on each slice.

Storage: Keep the cake tightly wrapped or in an airtight container for up to 5 days or freeze for up to 6 months.

Carrot-Walnut Cake with Caramel Cream Cheese Frosting

PREP TIME: 15 MINUTES | COOK TIME: 35 MINUTES | YIELD: 9 SERVINGS (1 PIECE PER SERVING)

THC: 5MG PER SERVING | VEGETARIAN

I love a moist carrot cake. You can almost make believe that you are eating something healthy. This recipe uses pineapple to add a bit of sweet and tart.

6½ tablespoons canola oil

1½ tablespoons Canna-Oil (page 47)

1 cup granulated sugar

2 large eggs, beaten

1 cup grated carrots

½ cup canned crushed pineapple, drained

½ teaspoon vanilla extract

1 cup all-purpose flour

1 teaspoon baking soda

½ teaspoon baking powder

½ teaspoon ground cinnamon

¾ cup walnuts, chopped

¾ cup caramel candy pieces, chopped

1 (8-ounce) package cream cheese, softened

½ cup confectioners' sugar

1 teaspoon vanilla extract

1. Preheat the oven to 340°F. Line the bottom and sides of an 8-inch square baking pan with parchment paper with an overhang on two sides.

2. In a large bowl, using a wooden spoon, combine the oils and granulated sugar. Stir in the eggs, carrots, pineapple, and vanilla.

3. In a medium bowl, stir together the flour, baking soda, baking powder, and cinnamon. Combine the dry mixture with the wet ingredients. Stir in the walnuts. Pour the batter into the prepared pan.

4. Bake until the top is nicely golden brown and the cake is starting to pull away from the pan along the edges, 33 to 35 minutes. Let the cake cool. It will slightly sink in the middle, but that's fine.

5. In a small bowl, melt the caramels with 1 tablespoon water in the microwave on medium power for 30-second intervals. Stir in between intervals until smooth.

6. In a medium bowl, using an electric mixer on medium speed, beat the cream cheese and confectioners' sugar together until light and fluffy. Stir in the melted caramel and vanilla. Once the cake is completely cooled, frost the cake with the caramel cream cheese frosting, cut into 9 equal pieces, and serve.

Storage: Keep the cake tightly wrapped in the refrigerator for 5 to 7 days. It can be frozen, unfrosted, for up to 6 months.

Chocolate Zucchini Bread

PREP TIME: 15 MINUTES | COOK TIME: 1 HOUR | YIELD: 9 SERVINGS (1 SLICE PER SERVING)

THC: 5MG PER SLICE | NUT-FREE | VEGETARIAN

The first time I tried zucchini bread, I was somewhat skeptical. Zucchini in a bread? Really? And then I tried it. So, let me tell you—yes, the zucchini brings a moistness to this tantalizing sweet, and the grated chocolate gilds the lily. Try it. You'll thank me.

Nonstick baking spray

1 cup all-purpose flour

½ cup Dutch process unsweetened cocoa powder

1 teaspoon baking soda

½ teaspoon ground cinnamon

¼ teaspoon ground ginger

¼ teaspoon salt

2 large eggs, at room temperature

1½ tablespoons Canna-Butter (page 43), melted and slightly cooled

2½ tablespoons unsalted butter, melted and slightly cooled

¼ cup canola or coconut oil, melted and cooled

¾ cup packed light brown sugar

1 teaspoon vanilla extract

1½ cups packed shredded zucchini, squeezed of liquid in a clean dish towel

4.5 ounces semisweet chocolate, grated (about 1 cup; see Tip), divided

1. Preheat the oven to 340°F. Coat an 8-inch loaf pan with nonstick spray.

2. In a medium bowl, whisk together the flour, cocoa, baking soda, cinnamon, ginger, and salt. Set aside.

3. In a large bowl, whisk the eggs, melted butters, oil, brown sugar, and vanilla together until smooth. You might have a few small brown sugar clumps—that's fine. Stir the dry ingredients into the wet ingredients; don't overmix. Stir in the zucchini until just combined. Stir three-quarters of the grated chocolate just until combined. Pour the batter into the prepared pan. Sprinkle the remaining grated chocolate evenly over the top.

4. Bake until a toothpick inserted into the center of the bread comes out mostly clean, 50 to 60 minutes. Let the bread cool in the pan on a wire rack for 15 minutes. Run a knife around the edges of the bread and carefully remove from the pan. Let the bread cool completely on the wire rack. Cut into 9 slices and serve.

Tip: Grab a semisweet chocolate bar and a vegetable peeler and scrape the peeler down the narrow edge of the bar over a bowl or plate to catch the chocolate. Grate the chocolate until you have about 1 cup. A peeler is so much easier to clean than a cheese grater—you're welcome!

Storage: Keep the loaf tightly wrapped in aluminum foil in the refrigerator for 4 to 5 days or freeze for up to 6 months.

Everything Yummy Cake Muffins

PREP TIME: 10 MINUTES | COOK TIME: 35 MINUTES | YIELD: 12 SERVINGS (1 MUFFIN PER SERVING)
THC: 5MG PER MUFFIN | VEGETARIAN

These muffins are moist and have a homey, inviting flavor. They are loaded with a range of textures and flavors, resulting in a rich cakey treat. Most of the time, I bake muffins and cupcakes in paper liners to prevent them from sticking. Sometimes nuts or dried fruit don't want to come out easily, and using paper liners makes that a nonissue.

Nonstick baking spray (optional)

2 large eggs

½ cup plus 2 tablespoons canola oil

2 tablespoons Canna-Oil (page 47)

¼ cup milk

1 cup all-purpose flour

1 cup whole wheat flour

1 cup packed light brown sugar

2 teaspoons baking soda

1 teaspoon ground cinnamon

½ teaspoon salt

1½ cups shredded carrots (2 to 3 carrots)

1½ cups shredded peeled apples

¾ cup chopped walnuts

½ cup shredded unsweetened coconut

½ cup raisins

1. Preheat the oven to 340°F. Line a standard muffin tin with paper liners or coat with nonstick spray.

2. In a large bowl, beat the eggs, oils, and milk together until well combined.

3. In a medium bowl, combine the flours, sugar, baking soda, cinnamon, and salt. Combine the egg mixture with the dry ingredients just until incorporated. Add the carrots, apples, walnuts, coconut, and raisins and mix well. Pour into the prepared pan.

4. Bake until a toothpick inserted in the center comes out clean, 30 to 35 minutes.

5. Allow to cool in the pan on a wire rack for at least 20 minutes before removing. Enjoy!

Storage: Keep the muffins tightly wrapped or in an airtight container for up to a week. They freeze very well for up to 6 months.

CANTALOUPE-LIME
POPS, PAGE 115

CHAPTER 8

Other Sweet Little Things

Move over cakes and cookies, these cannabis-infused treats hit the spot when you are looking for something infused that's a little different. Berries swathed in chocolate, bananas layered with custard and cookies, and frosty ice pops are all soul-satisfying, and these indulgences will likely become favorites. If you've never made or eaten a pavlova, give that recipe a try on a non-humid day. It's kind of marshmallow-like, has a terrific crunchy texture on the outside, and is soft and light on the inside. And since the raspberry sauce is the infused part, feel free to make it to spoon over any of the recipes in the book to double dose.

Chocolate-Dipped Strawberries

PREP TIME: 10 MINUTES | YIELD: 12 CHOCOLATE-DIPPED STRAWBERRIES | SERVINGS: 6 SERVINGS (2 STRAWBERRIES PER SERVING) | THC: 5MG PER SERVING (2.5MG PER STRAWBERRY) | GLUTEN-FREE NUT-FREE | VEGAN

We all know chocolate and strawberries pair beautifully—and look beautiful at that. Thankfully, this recipe is so incredibly simple and delicious. If you don't have ripe strawberries on hand, dip whatever you do have! Why not, right? If you don't have a double boiler, set a heat-safe bowl over a pan with a little water to improvise. These are best when made and eaten within a couple of hours.

1 tablespoon Canna-Coconut Oil (page 45)

1½ cups vegan chocolate chips

12 large strawberries, rinsed and patted dry

1. In a double boiler, melt the oil and chocolate over medium heat. Stir until smooth.

2. Dip the berries in the chocolate and place on parchment paper to set, at least 30 minutes.

Cantaloupe-Lime Pops

PREP TIME: 10 MINUTES PLUS 4 HOURS FREEZE TIME | YIELD: 6 SERVINGS (1 POP PER SERVING)

THC: 5MG PER POP | DAIRY-FREE | GLUTEN-FREE | NUT-FREE | VEGETARIAN

I always have ice pops in my freezer. So refreshing on a hot day, and they're a delightful treat on a rainy one. There is something wonderful about putting everything in a blender and letting her go, plus you can change up the flavor by substituting in different fruit for the cantaloupe (see the variations below). There are so many awesome popsicle shapes, and there are always little paper cups and popsicle sticks.

5 to 6 cups very ripe cantaloupe chunks

2 tablespoons honey

2 tablespoons orange juice concentrate

2 tablespoons freshly squeezed lime juice

2 tablespoons chopped fresh mint

1 tablespoon Canna-Coconut Oil (page 45)

1. In a blender, purée the cantaloupe chunks, honey, orange juice concentrate, lime juice, mint, and canna-coconut oil together until smooth.
2. Pour into popsicle molds and freeze until firm.
3. Remove the pops from the molds according to the manufacturer's instructions.

Storage: These refreshing pops will last for at least 6 months.

Variations: Honeydew-Lime Pops: Substitute honeydew chunks, omit the concentrate, and add the grated zest of 1 lime.
Pineapple Pops: Substitute pineapple chunks and omit the mint.
Watermelon Pops: Substitute seedless watermelon chunks and omit the concentrate and mint.

Nutty Banana Yogurt Pops

PREP TIME: 10 MINUTES PLUS 4 HOURS FREEZE TIME | YIELD: 6 SERVINGS (1 POP PER SERVING)

THC: 5MG PER POP | GLUTEN-FREE | VEGETARIAN

This recipe started out as a smoothie. It's such a terrific combination of flavors and it's healthy. Sometimes I add a bit of freshly grated nutmeg, a nice spicy touch. Freezing the banana before processing it yields a better final texture.

1½ cups vanilla yogurt

¼ cup unsweetened cocoa powder

1 tablespoon Canna-Coconut Oil (page 45)

1 ripe medium banana, sliced and frozen

1 tablespoon honey

½ cup chopped peanuts

1. In a blender, purée the yogurt, cocoa, canna-coconut oil, banana, and honey until smooth. Transfer the mixture to a medium bowl and stir in the peanuts.

2. Pour the mixture into popsicle molds and freeze until firm.

3. Remove the pops from the molds according to the manufacturer's instructions.

Storage: Keep the pops in an airtight container in the freezer for up to several months.

Banana Pudding Parfaits

PREP TIME: 45 MINUTES, PLUS 2 HOURS CHILL TIME | COOK TIME: 30 MINUTES | YIELD: 6 SERVINGS (1 PARFAIT PER SERVING) | THC: 5MG PER PARFAIT | NUT-FREE | VEGETARIAN

Banana pudding is a big favorite in our family. We've been making it for years, sans cannabis. This time around, we are creating the ultimate adult's banana puddings. These parfaits are best served the day they are made.

6 large egg yolks

¾ cup granulated sugar

¼ cup plus
2 tablespoons cornstarch

¼ heaping teaspoon salt

3½ cups whole milk

1 tablespoon unsalted
Canna-Butter (page 43)

1 tablespoon vanilla extract

1 tablespoon spiced rum

½ cup cold heavy cream

2 tablespoons
confectioners' sugar

2 cups broken
shortbread cookies

3 large ripe bananas, sliced

1. In a medium saucepan, stir together the egg yolks, granulated sugar, cornstarch, and salt over medium heat. Whisk in the milk and bring to a simmer, stirring frequently, 5 to 8 minutes. When the mixture starts to bubble, turn the heat down to low and continue cooking, whisking constantly, until the mixture thickens, 1 to 2 minutes.

2. Remove the pan from the heat and immediately whisk in the canna-butter, vanilla, and rum. Transfer the mixture to a bowl and place a piece of plastic wrap directly on the surface of the pudding to keep a film from forming. Refrigerate until cool, a few hours. (To hurry it up, you can place the bowl in a larger bowl filled with ice and whisk occasionally until cold.)

3. Once the pudding is cold, place the cream in a medium bowl. Using an electric mixer on medium-low speed, whip until the beaters begin to leave tracks in the cream. Add the confectioners' sugar and whip until the cream holds silky, medium-firm peaks. Go slowly toward the end; if it gets grainy or curdled, you've gone too far. Use a rubber spatula to fold the whipped cream into the cold pudding.

4. Into each of 6 parfait glasses, spoon a large dollop of the pudding mixture. Top with a layer of cookie pieces and a layer of sliced bananas. Repeat the layers and top with a final layer of pudding. Crumble some of the cookie pieces and sprinkle over the top. Refrigerate until ready to serve.

Tip: Do not slice the bananas until you are ready to assemble the parfaits.

Almond Matcha Truffles

PREP TIME: 10 MINUTES | YIELD: 10 TRUFFLES | SERVINGS: 5 SERVINGS (2 TRUFFLES PER SERVING)

THC: 5MG PER SERVING, 2.5MG PER TRUFFLE | GLUTEN-FREE | VEGAN

Matcha is powdered green tea. It's got a strong flavor, love it or hate it. And it's good for you, so there's that. A little goes a long way. And the color, pale green, is divine.

FOR THE TRUFFLES

7 dates, pitted

1 cup raw cacao powder

½ cup raw almond butter

2½ teaspoons Canna-Coconut Oil (page 45)

1 tablespoon vanilla extract

1 teaspoon matcha powder

½ teaspoon salt

FOR THE TOPPINGS (OPTIONAL)

Matcha powder

Pink rose powder

Crushed goji berries

Cacao powder

Crushed nuts

1. In a food processor, blend all the truffle ingredients together until the mixture has a crumbly texture. It may look really dry, but that's how it is supposed to look.

2. Place parchment paper on your work surface. Form the mixture into 1-inch balls. If it feels dry, just knead it as you would bread dough. Roll it between the palms of your hands.

3. Place your desired topping on a baking sheet with sides. Roll each truffle in the topping of your choice.

Storage: Keep the truffles in an airtight container in the refrigerator for up to 2 weeks or freeze for up to 6 months.

Pavlova with Canna-Raspberry Sauce

PREP TIME: 20 MINUTES | COOK TIME: 30 MINUTES | YIELD: 6 SERVINGS (1 PAVLOVA PER SERVING)

THC: 5MG PER PAVLOVA | DAIRY-FREE | GLUTEN-FREE | VEGETARIAN

Crispy on the outside but soft and chewy on the inside, these naturally gluten-free meringues are the perfect end to dinner. Best not to make them on a humid day; meringue is tricky.

FOR THE MERINGUES

3 large egg whites, at room temperature

½ teaspoon cream of tartar

Pinch salt

⅔ cup granulated sugar

2 teaspoons cornstarch

1 teaspoon white vinegar

1 teaspoon vanilla extract

FOR THE RASPBERRY SAUCE

½ cup orange juice

2 teaspoons cornstarch

1 pound raspberries, rinsed

¼ cup honey

1 tablespoon Canna-Coconut Oil (page 45)

Pinch salt

1. Preheat the oven to 275°F. Line a baking sheet with parchment paper.
2. For the meringues, in a tall, metal bowl, using an electric mixer on high speed, whip the egg whites, cream of tartar, and salt together until soft peaks form, about 1 minute.
3. With the mixer still running, slowly add the sugar, 2 tablespoons at a time. Continue to beat on high speed until stiff peaks form. If you feel the meringue between your fingers, it should be smooth. If you still feel the sugar granules, keep beating on medium speed until the sugar has fully dissolved. Add the cornstarch, vinegar, and vanilla and whisk to incorporate.
4. Spoon about ½ cup of the egg white mixture for each pavlova onto the prepared baking sheet. Using a spoon, spread each into a 3-inch concave circle, with higher sides and a slight hollow in the middle. You should have enough for 6 pavlovas.
5. Bake until very light tan in color and the meringue seems set, 25 to 30 minutes. Turn off the oven, open the door a smidge, and allow the pavlovas to cool completely.
6. For the raspberry sauce, in a small bowl, combine the orange juice and cornstarch. Stir to until smooth.

7. In a small saucepan over low heat, combine the raspberries, honey, and canna-oil and mix well, mashing the raspberries into a smooth sauce as they soften. Add the cornstarch mixture, increase the heat to medium, and stir until the mixture begins to thicken, 4 to 5 minutes; the sauce will continue to thicken as it cools. Stir in the salt. Remove from the heat and pour into a small pitcher.

8. Top the pavlovas with equal portions of the raspberry sauce immediately before serving.

Storage: You can prepare the pavlovas hours in advance and store them in an airtight container at room temperature until ready to serve. The sauce can also be made in advance and stored in the refrigerator, covered. If it is too thick to pour, heat it in the microwave for 10 seconds or so. Once sauced, you need to eat the pavlovas immediately.

Mason Jar Trifle Cups with Berries and Cake

PREP TIME: 10 MINUTES | YIELD: 6 TRIFLES | SERVINGS: 6 SERVINGS (1 TRIFLE PER SERVING)

THC: 5MG PER TRIFLE | NUT-FREE | VEGETARIAN

I love to make these trifles in Mason jars. So easy, so pretty, and so delicious. Instead of the traditional custard, which can be a bit of a pain, Greek yogurt is just as creamy, better for you, and totally delish. If you like, prepare this the day before, put the lids on the jars, and add the whipped cream when ready to serve.

1½ cups berries (quartered or sliced if using strawberries), plus extra for garnish

2 tablespoons honey

1½ cups cake crumbs, divided

1½ cups vanilla Greek yogurt

1 tablespoon Canna-Butter (page 43) or Canna-Oil (page 47), melted and cooled

Strawberry yogurt, for garnish

1. Place 6 Mason jars on your work surface. In a small bowl, mix the berries with the honey.
2. Reserve 3 tablespoons of the cake crumbs and divide the rest between the 6 jars. Sprinkle the berries over the cake crumbs.
3. In a small bowl, combine the vanilla yogurt with the canna-butter. Divide the yogurt evenly between the jars. Sprinkle with the reserved cake crumbs and top with a dollop of strawberry yogurt and a sprinkling of berries.

Tip: For the cake crumbs, use either your favorite recipe for pound cake, angel food cake, or biscuits, or use a store-bought pound cake, angel food cake, or biscuits. It's preferable to use day-old cake or biscuits for easier crumbling and structure within the trifle. Crumble the cake/biscuits into ½ to 1-inch size pieces, enough for 1½ cups.

Storage: Keep the trifles tightly covered in the refrigerator for up to 3 days.

Mini Apple Crisps

PREP TIME: 15 MINUTES | COOK TIME: 25 MINUTES | YIELD: 4 SERVINGS (1 CRISP PER SERVING)
THC: 5MG PER CRISP | VEGETARIAN

This Mason jar crisp is outstanding. The ginger gives the pie a depth of flavor you will adore. Feel free to switch the nuts to walnuts, my second favorite nut.

4 Granny Smith apples, cored, peeled, and sliced (around 4½ cups)

2 teaspoons minced peeled fresh ginger

½ teaspoon ground cinnamon

Pinch salt

⅓ cup honey

½ tablespoon balsamic vinegar

¾ cup old-fashioned rolled oats

⅓ cup all-purpose flour

¼ cup slivered almonds

¼ cup maple syrup

2 teaspoons Canna-Butter (page 43), melted or very soft

⅛ teaspoon salt

1. Preheat the oven to 340°F.
2. In a large skillet, mix the apples, ginger, cinnamon, and salt together. Stir in the honey and vinegar. Cook over low heat, stirring occasionally, until softened, about 15 minutes.
3. In a medium bowl, stir together the oats, flour, almonds, maple syrup, canna-butter, and salt.
4. Divide the fruit mixture between 4 half-pint Mason jars or ramekins. Spread the crumble over the fruit, pressing down on the crumbs to ensure that none are above the top of the jar or ramekin.
5. Place the jars or ramekins on a baking sheet and bake until the tops are brown, 20 to 25 minutes. Let cool for 10 minutes and enjoy.

Storage: Keep the crisps tightly covered in the refrigerator for up to 5 days. They freeze surprisingly well; defrost overnight in the refrigerator before reheating.

Graham Cracker, Peanut Butter, and Banana Sandwiches

PREP TIME: 10 MINUTES | YIELD: 2 SERVINGS (1 SANDWICH PER SERVING)

THC: 5MG PER SANDWICH | VEGAN

Whether you choose creamy or crunchy, peanut butter and bananas are such a great pair. Spread between graham crackers, it becomes a sandwich of sorts. This makes a great breakfast, snack, or dessert. Make it and eat it—this one doesn't keep.

4 double graham crackers

½ cup peanut butter

1 teaspoon Canna-Coconut Oil (page 45)

1 banana, sliced and tossed with 1 teaspoon lemon juice

2 tablespoons shredded unsweetened coconut

1. Place 2 double graham crackers on your work surface.
2. In a small bowl, mix the peanut butter and canna-coconut oil together and spread on each graham cracker.
3. Divide the sliced banana between the crackers.
4. Sprinkle with the coconut. Put the tops on and eat.

Hot Chocolate with Caramel

PREP TIME: 2 MINUTES | COOK TIME: 5 MINUTES | YIELD: 4 SERVINGS (1 CUP PER SERVING)

THC: 5MG PER CUP | GLUTEN-FREE | NUT-FREE | VEGETARIAN

Caramel and chocolate have been hanging together for years. And they are a lovely couple.

3 cups milk

1 cup half-and-half

¼ cup granulated sugar

6 ounces semisweet chocolate chips

2 teaspoons Canna-Butter (page 43)

1 teaspoon vanilla extract

4 caramel candy pieces, unwrapped

1. In a medium saucepan, heat the milk, half-and-half, and sugar together over medium-low heat until dissolved.

2. When the milk has heated up to serving temperature, add the chocolate and canna-butter and stir until melted. Remove from the heat and stir in the vanilla.

3. Pour into cups, add a caramel to each one, and serve.

Storage: Store any leftover hot chocolate, covered, in the refrigerator for up to 2 days. Reheat in the microwave or on the stovetop—or enjoy over ice!

References

Backes, Michael. *Cannabis Pharmacy: The Practical Guide to Medical Marijuana*. New York: Black Dog & Leventhal, 2017.

Casarett, David, MD. *Stoned: A Doctor's Case for Medical Marijuana*. New York: Current, 2015.

Hicks, John, MD. *The Medicinal Power of Cannabis: Using a Natural Herb to Heal Arthritis, Nausea, Pain, and Other Ailments*. New York: Skyhorse Publishing, 2015.

Rosenthal, Ed. *Beyond Buds: Marijuana Extracts—Hash, Vaping, Dabbing, Edibles, and Medicines*. Piedmont, CA: Quick American Archives, 2014.

Werner, Clint. *Marijuana Gateway to Health: How Cannabis Protects Us from Cancer and Alzheimer's Disease*. San Francisco: Dachstar Press, 2011.

Wolf, Laurie, and Mary Wolf. *The Medical Marijuana Dispensary*. Berkeley, CA: Althea Press, 2016.

Measurement Conversions

VOLUME EQUIVALENTS (LIQUID)

US STANDARD	US STANDARD (OUNCES)	METRIC (APPROXIMATE)
2 tablespoons	1 fl. oz.	30 mL
¼ cup	2 fl. oz.	60 mL
½ cup	4 fl. oz.	120 mL
1 cup	8 fl. oz.	240 mL
1½ cups	12 fl. oz.	355 mL
2 cups or 1 pint	16 fl. oz.	475 mL
4 cups or 1 quart	32 fl. oz.	1 L
1 gallon	128 fl. oz.	4 L

OVEN TEMPERATURES

FAHRENHEIT	CELSIUS (APPROXIMATE)
250°F	120°C
300°F	150°C
325°F	165°C
350°F	180°C
375°F	190°C
400°F	200°C
425°F	220°C
450°F	230°C

VOLUME EQUIVALENTS (DRY)

US STANDARD	METRIC (APPROXIMATE)
$1/8$ teaspoon	0.5 mL
¼ teaspoon	1 mL
½ teaspoon	2 mL
¾ teaspoon	4 mL
1 teaspoon	5 mL
1 tablespoon	15 mL
¼ cup	59 mL
$1/3$ cup	79 mL
½ cup	118 mL
$2/3$ cup	156 mL
¾ cup	177 mL
1 cup	235 mL
2 cups or 1 pint	475 mL
3 cups	700 mL
4 cups or 1 quart	1 L

WEIGHT EQUIVALENTS

US STANDARD	METRIC (APPROXIMATE)
½ ounce	15 g
1 ounce	30 g
2 ounces	60 g
4 ounces	115 g
8 ounces	225 g
12 ounces	340 g
16 ounces or 1 pound	455 g

Index

Acknowledgments

We are deeply grateful for all the doctors, researchers, patients, and advocates who came before us for leading cannabis legalization, decriminalization, and destigmatization efforts. Because of them, an ever-growing number of us can now enjoy cannabis safely, legally, and regularly.

Special thanks to Rowshan, Kim, Eric, and all the folks at Green Leaf Labs for their consistently amazing work and support over the last few years. Their expertise has been critical in the development of our edibles and techniques.

Thank you to all our wonderful staff at Laurie + MaryJane! You make each day brighter.

And to Bruce and Nick, our Wolf men, for their support from the beginning and for enduring the ongoing trials of edible taste testing.

A special thanks to lovely Claire for her help on this book.

Laurie thanks Mary, Mary thanks Laurie. We are now stuck in an infinite thanks loop.

About the Authors

Laurie Wolf and Mary Wolf are a mother and daughter-in-law team that runs the award-winning cannabis company Laurie + MaryJane. In addition to producing high-quality edibles for recreational cannabis dispensaries, they provide recipes and guidance for at-home edible creations. Mary began working with Laurie five years ago, creating a cannabis edible company and growing it from medical to recreational. Together with Laurie, they have a thriving line of cannabis and hemp edibles and have written several books on cooking with cannabis.

Laurie, a classically trained chef and graduate of the Culinary Institute of America, has been a food stylist, food editor, recipe developer, and cookbook author for over 30 years. She has been a regular contributor and edible recipe developer for *Culture*, *Kitchen Toke*, *The Cannabist*, *High Times*, *Oregon Leaf*, *GreenState*, and *Cannabis Now*. She is a leading voice in cannabis edibles. Laurie's passion for cannabis as treatment stems from her exposure to her father's end-of-life care as well as her own successful management of a seizure disorder.